DIABETES

BARBARA GOODHEART

DIABETES

Franklin Watts
New York / London / Toronto / Sydney / 1990
A Venture Book

Diagrams by Vantage Art

Photographs courtesy of: The Bettmann Archive: p. 12; World Health
Organization: pp.20 (Best Institute), 22 (J.P. Assal); Monkmeyer Photo:
p. 38 (Mimi Forsyth); Photo Researchers: pp. 43 (Grapes/Michaud), 55,
85 bottom (all Martin Dohrn), 58 (S.I.U.), 85 top (Fred McConnaughey),
86 (Don Kryminec), 87 (Science Photo Library); Juvenile Diabetes
Foundation/Nelson Bakerman: pp. 63, 75; Taurus Photos: p. 96 (M. Rotker);
National Baseball Hall of Fame and Museum: p. 103; UPI/Bettmann: p. 110.

616.462
$G00$

Library of Congress Cataloging-in-Publication Data

Goodheart, Barbara.
Diabetes / Barbara Goodheart.
p. cm.—(A Venture book)
Includes bibliographical references.
Summary: Looks at the condition of diabetes, what is necessary
for a diabetic to maintain proper health, what must be done in the
event of an insulin reaction, and the possibilities of a cure.
ISBN 0-531-10882-1
1. Diabetes—Juvenile literature. [1. Diabetes.] I. Title.
RC660.5.G66 1990
616.4'62—dc20 90-31328 CIP AC

96443

CONTENTS

DIABETES

INTRODUCTION

Amy is a peppy fourteen-year-old who loves ice skating and gymnastics. Kevin, who's seventeen and lives near the ocean, is into snorkeling and surfing. Both are active, happy kids. And both have *diabetes*.

Amy and Kevin give themselves insulin shots every day. They also use special tests to check how much sugar they have in their blood. But otherwise their lives aren't very different from those of other young people. They eat many of the foods others do—but reserve sweets such as cake, pie, and ice cream for special occasions.

Diabetes is a disease that prevents the body from getting energy from food in the usual way. Normally, much of the food we eat is turned into a simple sugar called *glucose*. With the help of a *hormone* called *insulin,* glucose enters the body cells and is used for energy.

When someone has diabetes, the body doesn't produce insulin or insulin doesn't work the way it should. Because of the problem with insulin, cells cannot properly absorb glucose (sugar) from the blood, and high levels of glucose build up in the blood. As the kidneys filter the blood, they pass some of the glucose into the urine. The person becomes extremely hungry and thirsty, drinks lots of water, and has to go to the bathroom very often. Over many years, high sugar levels in the blood can cause harmful effects called *complications*. These include diseases of the eyes, kidneys, blood vessels, and nerves.

Today almost twelve million Americans have diabetes, or about one person in twenty. Almost half of them aren't even aware that they have it.

What causes diabetes? How is it treated? Can it be prevented?

This book will answer many of your questions. We'll start with the history of diabetes—and the exciting story of how insulin was discovered.

large amounts of sugary urine, the term *diabetes mellitus* was created by adding the Latin word for "sweet" or "honeyed" to the original Greek word.

According to folklore, the ancients had a primitive but effective way of diagnosing diabetes. They simply poured the patient's urine on the ground near an anthill. If ants swarmed to the urine, it meant that sugar was present and the patient had diabetes.

Not until near the end of the eighteenth century did doctors begin to really learn something about diabetes. In 1776, a British doctor named Matthew Dobson tasted blood from a diabetic patient and found that it was sweet. He then used chemical tests to prove that the urine of diabetic patients contains sugar. Dobson also showed that sugar is present in the **blood** of both diabetic and healthy people, and he suggested that in diabetic people sugar somehow passes from the blood into the urine. Dobson was correct, but many years passed before other scientists realized the importance of his work.

In the mid-nineteenth century the famous French scientist Claude Bernard discovered that sugar can be stored in the liver in a form called *glycogen*. He also demonstrated that the body can break down glycogen into the sugar we now know as glucose and pass it

Aretaeus was a Greek physician and writer who described many diseases and conditions, including diabetes.

directly into the blood. Bernard was the first to show that an organ can make a substance and secrete it directly into the bloodstream.

Langerhans's Discovery

In 1869, a German medical student named Paul Langerhans used a microscope to study tissue from the *pancreas,* a gland behind the stomach (see Figure 1). At the time, the pancreas was known to contain cells that secrete substances called *enzymes.* It was also known that these enzymes pass through a duct from the pancreas into the intestine, where they help break down food during digestion.

Using special stains on his microscope specimens, Langerhans found groups of cells scattered like tiny islands throughout the pancreas. These cell islands (islets) had never been described, and Langerhans had no idea of their function. Today we know that among the cells in the *islets of Langerhans,* named after their discoverer, are the *beta cells,* which produce insulin.

Minkowski's Work

Twenty years after Langerhans's discovery, Oskar Minkowski and Joseph von Mering, working in France, studied the role of the pancreas in fat digestion. As part of their work, they removed the pancreas of a laboratory dog. They were startled when the previously housebroken dog lost bladder control and urinated repeatedly on the floor.

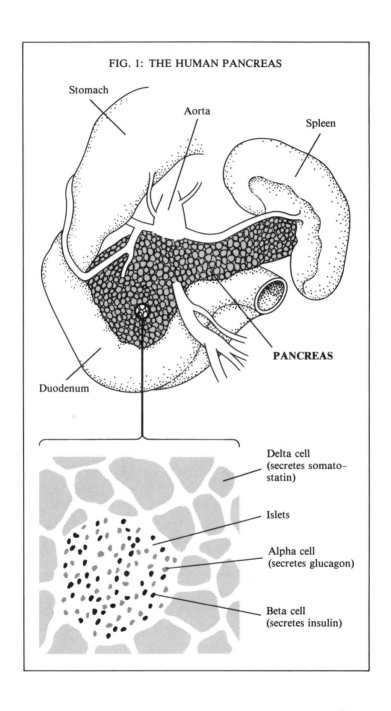

FIG. 1: THE HUMAN PANCREAS

Stomach

Aorta

Spleen

PANCREAS

Duodenum

Delta cell
(secretes somato-
statin)

Islets

Alpha cell
(secretes glucagon)

Beta cell
(secretes insulin)

Acting on a hunch, Minkowski tested the dog's urine for sugar and found that the animal had developed severe diabetes. This important discovery led him to wonder if diabetes in humans is linked in some way to a problem involving the pancreas.

Additional studies suggested to Minkowski and others that diabetes is caused by the lack of a hormone from the pancreatic islets—a hormone needed to control blood sugar levels. If so, they reasoned, tissue from a normal pancreas would contain the hormone. Extracting the tissue with a solution similar to body fluid would yield a preparation that might contain the hormone, which could then be used to treat diabetic patients.

But obtaining the active material—the hormone we now know as insulin—proved difficult. Preparations given by mouth failed to work because the digestive enzymes that break down food also destroy insulin. Some preparations even made patients violently ill. After many failures, it seemed that if the mysterious hormone actually existed—and many doubted that it did—perhaps it couldn't be extracted and used in patients.

Bloodletting, Doping, and Starving

While laboratory research continued, doctors could do little to help diabetic patients. Bloodletting, thought to have curative powers, was found to be useless. Opium, a narcotic drug that relieves pain, was used to slow body function when diabetes worsened. Opium may have dulled patients' despair, but it failed to prolong life.

Diets for diabetic patients were generally low in carbohydrates and high in proteins and fats. A popular diet, devised in 1797 and widely used for decades, was as follows.

Breakfast and Supper:	1½ pints milk and ½ pint limewater, mixed; bread and butter
Lunch:	Pudding made of blood and suet
Dinner:	Game, or fat and rancid old meats, which have been long hung; as fat as the stomach can bear

As bad as this fare must have been, patients probably preferred it to the semistarvation diets that were briefly popular in the late 1800s and early 1900s.

These diets were high in carbohydrates—the "potato cure," the "oat cure" (oatmeal gruel), and "the rice cure." Some unfortunate patients were locked in their rooms for weeks or months so they wouldn't eat forbidden food. A common program consisted of several days of starvation (which lowered blood sugar levels to normal), followed by a low-carbohydrate, low-calorie diet.

Such diets were sometimes useful in older patients who were mildly ill, but nothing helped for long when the patient was a severely ill child. These children lost weight and became weak, emaciated, and despondent. Near the end they resembled prisoners in a death camp. When a patient's breath developed a sweetish odor, like the smell of rotting apples, the family knew there was no hope. The patient soon fell into a *coma,* gasping for air. Most young patients with diabetes died less than a year after becoming ill.

The Discovery of Insulin

While doctors continued to prescribe diets, dedicated scientists tried to find some way to treat diabetes. Many had seen the terrible consequences of the disease in their own friends or loved ones.

In the early 1900s, several studies rekindled interest in a possible link between diabetes and lack of a secretion from the islets of Langerhans. In 1920, a young Canadian surgeon who had become intrigued by stories of the mysterious secretion sought funds to do research. Although Frederick Banting was soon to make one of the most important discoveries in the history of medicine, no one at the time was interested in supporting an unknown surgeon's work.

In 1921, Banting arranged to spend his summer vacation performing diabetes research in a small borrowed laboratory at the University of Toronto. He teamed up with a young medical student named Charles Best. Working long hours without pay, Banting and Best set out to solve the mystery that had stymied hundreds of renowned scientists for so many years. Their plan was to work with laboratory animals to destroy the enzyme-producing cells of the pancreas.

This would leave only the "magic islands," from which they hoped the hormone could be extracted.

Using laboratory dogs left over from other scientists' studies, Banting and Best tied the animals' pancreatic duct, the tube that carries digestive enzymes from the pancreas to the intestine. They reasoned that tying the duct should prevent the enzyme-producing cells of the pancreas from functioning. Those cells would not produce their secretion, and would waste away. But the islet cells, which secrete their hormone directly into the blood, should remain healthy. Banting and Best planned to prepare an extract from the islet cells and test it in diabetic dogs whose pancreas had been removed. If the extract contained the hormone, it would control the dogs' diabetes.

The laboratory work was far from glamorous. The animals needed to be fed, watered, bathed, and cared for, and their cages required frequent cleaning. Blood and urine samples had to be collected and analyzed in the laboratory.

During many weeks of hard work, the two scientists faced failure after failure. Many dogs died after surgery. Others were felled by infection and intolerable heat. Some dogs survived, but the pancreatic duct had been tied too loosely to destroy the enzyme-producing cells.

But Banting and Best were determined to reach their goal. Eventually they succeeded in tying off the pancreas, and at the end of July they carefully prepared an extract and injected it into a diabetic dog. To their delight, the dog's blood sugar levels dropped and the animal started to improve.

But much remained to be done. Working night and day, Banting and Best repeated their studies, checked their findings, and adjusted the doses of insulin used to treat the dogs. When one of the dogs lived several weeks, it seemed that the treatment at last was working.

When it was time to try treating a patient, Banting and Best first tested the safety of their insulin preparation by giving each other an injection. The insulin caused a little redness and swelling, but no serious effects. Since neither scientist was diabetic, there was no way to know if the insulin would control the symptoms of diabetes in human beings, as it had in dogs.

Less than six months after the first dog had been treated, insulin was injected into a patient. He was a fourteen-year-old boy named Leonard Thompson. When Leonard received his first shot, on January 11, 1922, he was terribly weak and near death. His blood sugar dropped after the injection, but a mild reaction

Dr. Frederick Banting and Dr. Charles Best pose in 1921 with the first dog to be kept alive with insulin. Their discovery is considered to be one of the most important revelations of modern medicine.

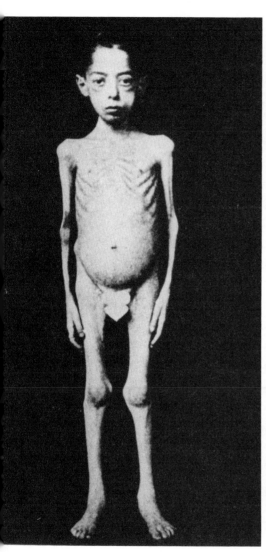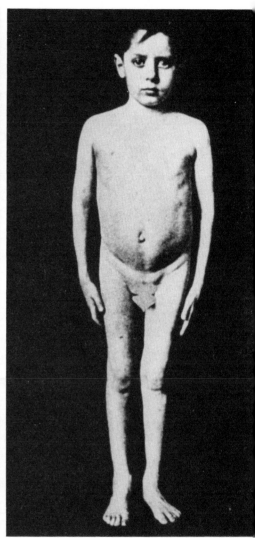

Fourteen-year-old Leonard Thompson
is shown before and after he received
insulin treatment. These photographs
were taken only two months apart.

followed. It was clear that the insulin preparation needed to be improved and larger quantities produced. Others at the University of Toronto, especially Professor J. J. R. Macleod and Dr. J. B. Collip, helped make the extract more active and less toxic.

Twelve days after his first injection, Leonard began receiving daily shots. He improved dramatically and soon resumed a normal life.

As word of Banting and Best's work spread throughout the world, other patients began receiving insulin treatment. Almost overnight the outlook for young diabetic patients changed dramatically. Just a few weeks of treatment transformed skeletal, emaciated young patients into healthy, plump-cheeked children. Once doomed to early death, children with diabetes could now look forward to a long life. In the many years since Banting and Best's discovery, insulin has saved the lives of millions of people.

For the discovery of insulin, Dr. Frederick Banting and Professor J. J. R. Macleod shared the 1923 Nobel Prize for medicine. Banting gave half his prize money to Best, declaring that Best deserved equal credit for the discovery. Macleod gave half his prize money to Dr. Collip.

CHAPTER

2

WHAT IS DIABETES?

"Diabetes" is a general term for disorders in which the body produces large amounts of urine. When the word "diabetes" is used alone, as in this book, it refers to diabetes mellitus. You may have heard of a different disease called *diabetes insipidus*. This disease is usually caused by lack of a hormone produced by the *pituitary gland*. People with diabetes insipidus pass large amounts of urine, but the urine is sugar-free.

In diabetes mellitus, something goes wrong with the body's metabolism of food. But before you can understand how diabetes develops, you'll need to know how the body normally uses food for energy.

Carbohydrates, Proteins, and Fats

When you swim across a pool, run to catch a bus, or even just think about what you're going to do next, your body uses energy. Where does this energy come from?

The food we eat contains three important sources of energy: carbohydrates (sugars and starches), proteins (meat, fish, and poultry), and fats. When food is digested, each of these substances is broken down into its smaller units, or "building blocks," and absorbed into the bloodstream. Carbohydrates are broken down into the body's quickest source of energy— the simple sugar called glucose. Proteins are mostly broken down into amino acids. The body uses amino acids in three major ways. Some are used as building blocks to repair tissue and to form new tissue. Some are changed into fat and stored for later use as an energy source. And some are changed into glucose by the liver.

Most of the fat from food is either stored in fat cells or broken down into fatty acids and other fats and then used for fuel. Between meals, when glucose is no longer readily available, fats are the body's main source of energy.

What Does Insulin Do?

As glucose is absorbed into the bloodstream, the amount of sugar in the blood quickly rises. In response, the beta cells in the pancreas secrete insulin into the bloodstream.

Insulin circulating in the blood attaches to *insulin receptor sites,* which are special places on the wall of each cell. When insulin binds to these sites, the cell "door" opens. Glucose then enters the cell and is used for energy. Thus, we can think of insulin as the "key" that allows glucose to enter the cell, and the receptor site as the "keyhole" into which insulin fits. An important exception is the brain cells. Glucose can enter brain cells without the help of insulin.

The body uses glucose in three important ways. Some is immediately oxidized ("burned") by the cells for energy. Some is stored as glycogen in liver and muscle tissue and later used for energy. And some is changed by the liver into fat and stored in fat cells. Glucose and fat cannot be stored for later use unless insulin is present.

Other Hormones

Between meals, blood sugar levels drop and the pancreas secretes less insulin. Other hormones take over, ensuring that blood sugar levels remain within a very narrow range. These hormones are *glucagon*, from the *alpha cells* of the islets; epinephrine and cortisol, from the adrenal glands; and growth hormone, from the pituitary gland.

These hormones can raise blood sugar in two ways. They cause the liver to turn glycogen back into glucose, and they stimulate the liver to form moderate amounts of glucose from amino acids and fats. Glucose is then released into the bloodstream and blood sugar levels rise slightly. The pancreas responds by playing its role in fine-tuning, producing enough insulin to keep blood sugar levels within a well-controlled range. Figure 2 illustrates the mechanisms that influence blood sugar levels.

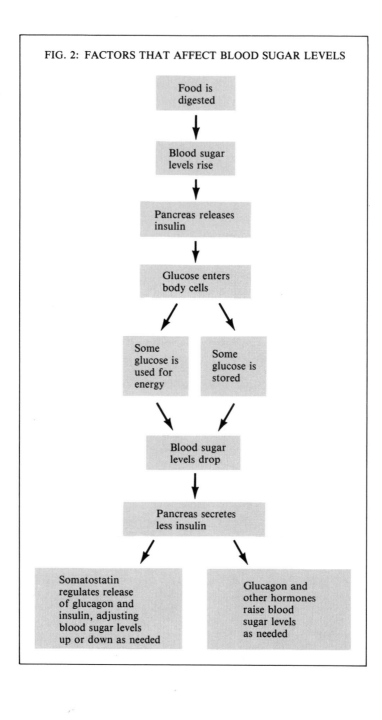

FIG. 2: FACTORS THAT AFFECT BLOOD SUGAR LEVELS

Food is digested

Blood sugar levels rise

Pancreas releases insulin

Glucose enters body cells

Some glucose is used for energy

Some glucose is stored

Blood sugar levels drop

Pancreas secretes less insulin

Somatostatin regulates release of glucagon and insulin, adjusting blood sugar levels up or down as needed

Glucagon and other hormones raise blood sugar levels as needed

Somatostatin, a hormone produced by the *delta cells* of the islets, also plays an important regulatory role. It regulates the release of glucagon and insulin, adjusting blood sugar levels up or down as needed.

Normally, the interplay among these hormones keeps blood sugar levels within a fairly narrow range, no matter what food is eaten or how active the person may be. This range is about 60 to 150 milligrams of glucose per deciliter *(mg/dL)* of plasma, the liquid part of the blood. At these levels the kidneys remove only very small amounts of sugar from the blood and pass it into the urine.

What Happens Without Insulin?

When the body doesn't have enough insulin, it can't use or store food for energy in the normal way. Glucose is locked out of the cells and builds up in the blood. Lacking insulin, the liver produces too much glucose. The kidneys "spill" some of the excess sugar into the urine.

Abnormal glucose metabolism is the most obvious change caused by lack of insulin. Metabolism of proteins and fats is also disrupted, however. Unable to use glucose, the body breaks down fat, fatty acids, and protein.

Abnormal metabolism of fats and proteins produces energy, but has harmful effects (see Figure 3). When fatty acids are broken down, waste products called *ketones* are formed. The body cannot remove large amounts of ketones from the blood. If the con-

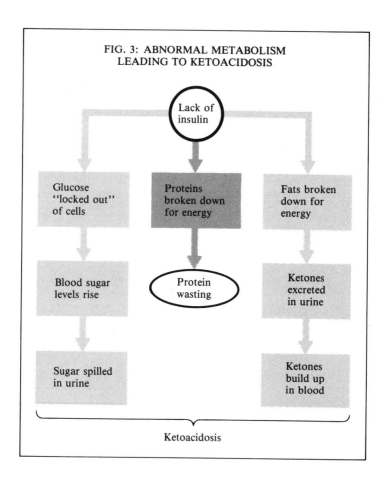

FIG. 3: ABNORMAL METABOLISM
LEADING TO KETOACIDOSIS

Lack of insulin

Glucose "locked out" of cells

Proteins broken down for energy

Fats broken down for energy

Blood sugar levels rise

Protein wasting

Ketones excreted in urine

Sugar spilled in urine

Ketones build up in blood

Ketoacidosis

centration of ketones becomes very high, a dangerous condition called *ketoacidosis* results.

Abnormal fat metabolism also speeds an aging process called *atherosclerosis*, in which fat deposits build up in the walls of the arteries. This buildup can interfere with the flow of blood. Atherosclerosis can result in heart attacks, strokes, and other health problems.

Abnormal protein metabolism can lead to a serious condition called protein wasting. Without insulin, protein is no longer formed or stored in the body and used in tissue formation and repair. Instead, existing protein is broken down. Protein wasting can cause extreme weakness, poor resistance to infection, and significant weight loss. It can also curtail normal growth in children.

CHAPTER

3

TYPES OF DIABETES

When twelve-year-old Kevin developed diabetes, he became terribly hungry and thirsty, although he ate huge meals and drank lots of milk and water. He also went to the bathroom very often. His mother worried because he was losing weight and was tired and weak.

Kevin had the classic signs and symptoms of diabetes: high blood sugar levels *(hyperglycemia)*, frequent urination *(polyuria)*, increased thirst *(polydipsia)*, and increased appetite or eating *(polyphagia)*. His urine contained sugar *(glycosuria)* and ketones *(ketonuria)*.

Now that you know how diabetes develops, you can understand Kevin's symptoms. He wasn't getting the energy he needed from his food, so he lost weight and felt hungry and tired. His body made extra urine to "wash away" the extra sugar in his blood, so Kevin

DECODING MEDICAL TERMS

Medical words sometimes seem to be part of another language! But with a few clues you can figure out what they mean.

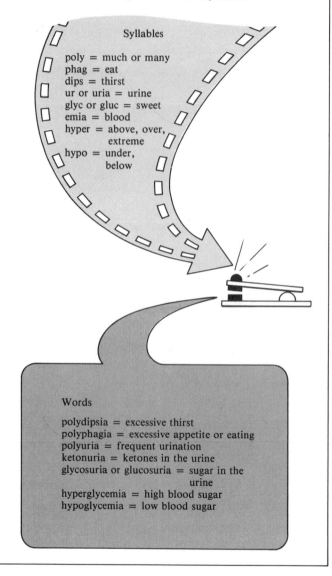

Syllables

poly = much or many
phag = eat
dips = thirst
ur or uria = urine
glyc or gluc = sweet
emia = blood
hyper = above, over, extreme
hypo = under, below

Words

polydipsia = excessive thirst
polyphagia = excessive appetite or eating
polyuria = frequent urination
ketonuria = ketones in the urine
glycosuria or glucosuria = sugar in the urine
hyperglycemia = high blood sugar
hypoglycemia = low blood sugar

went to the bathroom many times each day. His body lost too much water, making him terribly thirsty. Lack of insulin had caused all of Kevin's symptoms.

Kevin has *Type I, or insulin-dependent, diabetes mellitus (IDDM)*.

What Is Type I Diabetes?

About 10 to 20 percent of people with diabetes mellitus have Type I, formerly called juvenile-onset diabetes. Type I occurs most often in children and young adults, but can arise at any age.

In Type I, the pancreas produces little or no insulin. The disease usually begins suddenly, and the symptoms are severe. Because everyone needs insulin to live, people like Kevin normally have to take insulin injections every day for the rest of their lives. This is why Type I is called "insulin-dependent" diabetes. Insulin can control Type I, but does not cure it.

Most people with Type I are not overweight, but they need to be careful about the type of food they eat, when they eat, and how much they eat. This helps keep their blood sugar levels within normal range. They also need to stay physically active because sports and other physical activities lower blood sugar levels and help insulin work more effectively.

What Is Type II Diabetes?

Maria is obese (seriously overweight). She didn't know she had diabetes until a routine checkup showed high sugar levels in her blood and sugar in her urine. Unfortunately, her diabetes had already caused kidney disease.

About 80 to 90 percent of people with diabetes mellitus have *Type II,* or *non-insulin-dependent diabetes mellitus (NIDDM).* Although Type II was formerly called adult- or maturity-onset diabetes, it can arise at any age. The disease usually develops slowly, and symptoms tend to be mild.

But Type II is not a mild disease. Like Type I, it can lead to serious long-term complications.

Most people who develop Type II are over age forty, overweight, and inactive. They also have relatives with the disease.

Surprisingly, most people with Type II actually produce normal or high amounts of insulin. How do we know this? In 1950, Dr. Rosalyn Yalow and her colleagues in New York City developed a clever way to measure the tiny amounts of insulin in the blood. They discovered that some people with diabetes have no insulin (Type I), while others have low, normal or even high amounts (Type II). Until that time, doctors thought that diabetes was always caused by lack of insulin. The new findings indicated that diabetes can be caused by lack of *effective* insulin as well as by lack of *enough* insulin. For her work, Dr. Yalow shared the 1977 Nobel Prize in medicine.

New studies have shown that many obese people with Type II have a significant reduction in the number of insulin receptors on the cell surfaces. In addition, the remaining receptors do not handle insulin normally. Many researchers believe that the problem in such patients is not lack of insulin, but the inability of the receptors to allow insulin to enter the cells— a matter of "insulin resistance." In contrast, most slender people with Type II do not produce enough insulin.

The key to controlling obese Type II diabetes is losing weight through diet and exercise. When extra weight is lost, the number and function of insulin receptors usually return to normal, and as a result blood sugar levels drop to normal range. If diet therapy fails to control blood sugar levels, *oral hypoglycemic drugs* may be necessary. Some people with Type II even need insulin injections to help control symptoms of diabetes, especially during illness, surgery, infection, or pregnancy, but they do not need injections in order to live. After several years, a small percentage of Type II patients become dependent on insulin to survive. They are then reclassified as Type I patients.

Varieties

Many people do not really fit in either the Type I or the Type II groups. Some seem to have a combination of Type I and Type II, while others appear to switch from one type to another. Some children who develop diabetes never need insulin. In other rare cases, patients experience severe insulin-dependent diabetes for a time yet later no longer require insulin to live. Some middle-aged people diagnosed with diabetes need insulin therapy immediately in order to survive. Perhaps there are several forms of Type II, involving different hereditary factors.

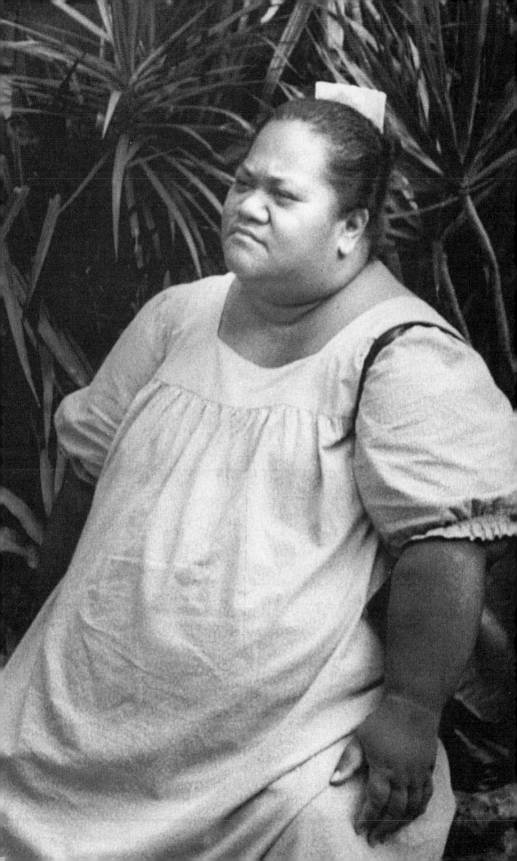

What Causes Diabetes?

You can't "catch" diabetes, and if you have it you can't give it to someone. Nor can you get diabetes as a result of something you've done—like eating too many sweets. Why, then, do some people become diabetic?

People can inherit a *tendency* toward diabetes, but not the disease itself. The tendency is acquired through *genes,* the basic units of heredity. It is through genes that characteristics such as brown eyes and dark hair are passed from parents to child. Although genes play a major role in determining who will get diabetes, the disease will not develop unless other conditions, or "triggering factors," occur.

The hereditary and triggering factors are different in Types I and II. This means that if Type II runs in your family, the risk of developing Type II is increased for you and other family members, but not the risk of developing Type I. Likewise, a family with a tendency toward Type I has no increased risk for developing Type II.

Studies show that many obese Type II diabetics suffer from "insulin resistance," which is an inability, or lack, of insulin receptors to allow the body's cells to take in insulin.

Causes of Type I

Three factors seem to interact in a complicated way in causing Type I: hereditary factors (the genetic tendency), immune factors, and "triggering" factors, such as viruses or stress.

Researchers believe that to develop Type I, a person needs to inherit the genetic tendency from both parents. Many people who carry the tendency are unaware of it, for only a very small percentage actually develop Type I. Consequently, many children with Type I have no history of the disease on either side of the family.

Even if Type I is known to run in the family, the risk that a family member will come down with it is relatively low. Doctors say that if one parent has Type I, the risk that a child will also have it is less than 10 percent. If both parents have Type I, the risk is less than 50 percent. If one identical twin has Type I diabetes, chances are only about 50 percent that the other twin—who has the identical genetic makeup—will eventually have it. Clearly, factors other than heredity play an important role.

It seems that in people with the genetic tendency, Type I can be triggered—but not directly caused—by environmental factors. In some cases viruses seem to be responsible. Infections with certain viruses such as Coxsackie B have been followed by Type I, and about 20 percent of babies born with German measles later come down with Type I. But it's clear that most children who have a viral disease do not become diabetic as a result.

Other cases of Type I appear to result from toxins. A group of people in a well-known study developed diabetes after eating tainted meat. Analysis showed that the meat contained a chemical toxin that destroys beta cells.

The body's immune system, which helps protect against infection, apparently plays an essential role in Type I. When bacteria, viruses, or other *antigens* invade the body, the immune system normally produces *antibodies* against them. The antibodies recognize the specific antigens and signal the body's defense system to destroy them. The immune system also forms antibodies against harmful substances produced within the body, such as toxins formed during disease states.

Normally the body recognizes and does not attack its own proteins. But sometimes something goes awry, so that the immune system perceives certain cells or other normal components of the body as being "foreign," and attacks them.

Apparently this is what happens in Type I. The body destroys its own beta cells as if they were foreign invaders. Scientists believe that about 90 percent of people with Type I have inherited certain *HLA antigens,* which are proteins on the surface of the body cells. These antigens help the immune system distinguish between the body's own tissues and foreign tissues. It's possible that the inherited HLA antigens in question, HLA-DR3 and -DR4, make the beta cells seem foreign, prompting the immune system to attack them. Yet this is not the entire answer, for some people with Type I do not have these antigens, and some people who have them do not develop Type I.

Scientists also know that long before someone

(41)

develops symptoms of Type I, one or more of three immune system antibodies, or "markers," appear in the blood. These antibodies, which destroy the beta cells, are known as islet cell antibodies (ICA), insulin autoantibodies (IAA), and antibodies against a specific protein of the islet cells (64K antibodies). While most people with Type I have no insulin-secreting beta cells, they do have normal amounts of other islet cells.

Causes of Type II
The tendency toward Type II diabetes is strongly linked with heredity. If one identical twin has Type II, chances are about 95 percent that the other twin will develop it. Hispanics, blacks, and Native Americans are especially at risk of Type II. It's not known whether these people are susceptible because of heredity or as a result of diet or other environmental factors.

Type II is not linked with the HLA antigens or with ICA, IAA, or 64K antibodies. It's been suggested that the genetic factor involved in Type II may be a mutation (change) in the insulin gene or the insulin receptor gene. And while the trigger in Type I seems to be a virus or other environmental factor, obesity appears to be the trigger in almost all people with Type II.

What role does obesity play? When someone is obese, the body has trouble using its insulin. If a person who hasn't inherited the tendency toward Type II gains too much weight, the body can make up for it by producing extra insulin. But if someone who has inherited the tendency becomes obese, he or she may develop Type II instead.

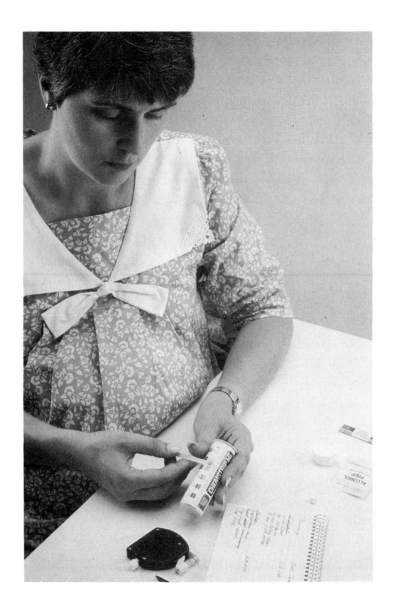

A pregnant woman with gestational diabetes compares test results of glucose in her blood with a chart.

Why does this happen? Scientists think that obesity may interfere with the cells' ability to use insulin, or may reduce the number of insulin receptors. Whatever the mechanism, most people with obese Type II can lower their blood sugar levels to normal range by losing extra weight and keeping it off. Some doctors even consider these people "cured." And most cases of obese Type II can be prevented if people with a family history of the disease kept their weight within normal range.

Other Types of Diabetes

Gestational diabetes is a term used when high blood sugar levels are found during pregnancy. Usually blood sugar levels return to normal after the baby is born, but about 25 to 50 percent of the mothers later develop Type II diabetes as a result of the pregnancy. Secondary diabetes arises when disease, drugs, or chemicals damage the pancreas or certain other organs, interfering with insulin production.

Impaired Glucose Tolerance

Impaired glucose tolerance was once called chemical, latent, or borderline diabetes. It is no longer considered a form of diabetes. In impaired glucose tolerance, blood sugar levels vary between normal and diabetic range. People with this condition can help protect themselves from diabetes by following a diet and physical activity program and by losing any excess weight.

CHAPTER

4

DIAGNOSIS

Remember the last time you had a checkup? The doctor examined you, asked questions, and ran some tests. The nurse took some blood from the tip of your finger or the large vein in your arm, and you gave a urine sample.

Let's see what happens when a doctor diagnoses diabetes.

Type I

For several weeks Michael, a ninth-grader, had been drinking a lot of water and getting up at night to go to the bathroom. Once he even wet the bed. One day Mike vomited in the school lunchroom, and that afternoon his mother took him to see his pediatrician.

Mike told Dr. McGivins that until a few days earlier he'd been hungry all the time. His mother said he'd been eating "like an orangutan"—yet he'd lost six pounds since his last visit. The kids were calling him "Skinny."

Tests revealed that Mike's blood sugar levels were much too high—over 300 mg/dL. His urine contained not only sugar but ketones, the waste products formed when fats are broken down for energy. Mike's symptoms and test results showed that he had Type I diabetes.

Type II

Mr. Gordon, age fifty-two, visited his doctor for a checkup. He was overweight and felt tired. Mr. Gordon's lab tests showed high blood sugar levels—220 mg/dL. His urine contained sugar but no ketones. His symptoms and test results indicated Type II diabetes (see Figure 4).

Blood Tests for Diagnosing Diabetes

Usually diabetes is diagnosed using either the fasting plasma glucose test or the random plasma glucose test. In the fasting plasma glucose test, the patient eats nothing overnight and the next morning a blood sample is taken from a vein in the inner arm. The amount of glucose in the plasma—the liquid part of the blood—is measured.

Fasting plasma glucose levels that are considered

FIG. 4: WARNING SIGNS OF DIABETES

Insulin-Dependent	Non-Insulin-Dependent
• frequent urination	• any of the insulin-dependent symptoms
• excessive thirst	• blurred vision or any change in sight
• extreme hunger	• tingling or numbness in legs, feet, or fingers
• sudden weight loss	
• weakness and fatigue	• slow healing of cuts (especially on the feet)
• irritability	• frequent skin infections or itchy skin
• nausea and vomiting	• drowsiness

"normal" vary with the type of test and with the person's age, overall health, medicine intake, and other factors. In general, a fasting plasma glucose level under 130 mg/dL for a child and under 115 mg/dL for an adult is considered normal. Diabetes is considered to be present in someone with typical symptoms of diabetes and a fasting plasma glucose level over 140 mg/dL. If symptoms are absent, a level of 140 mg/dL or higher on more than one occasion indicates that a person has diabetes.

Sometimes plasma glucose levels are measured randomly—without concern for mealtimes—rather than after a fast. When someone has symptoms of diabe-

(47)

tes, a random test showing a very high blood sugar level, over 200 mg/dL, indicates diabetes.

If glucose levels are not clearly normal or abnormal, a special test called an oral glucose tolerance test (OGTT) can be performed, but this is rarely necessary. In the OGTT, the patient fasts overnight and a blood sample is taken the next morning. The patient is then given a sugary drink. Additional blood samples are taken over the next several hours as the body breaks down the sugar. If the person does not have diabetes, the blood sugar level rises rapidly after the sweet drink, then falls quickly. If diabetes is present, levels rise higher than normal and fall slowly. If levels are above 200 mg/dL at two hours after the sugary drink and at one earlier point, diabetes is present.

CHAPTER

5

TREATMENT

The goal in treating diabetes is to keep blood sugar levels within or near nondiabetic range. This will help the body use carbohydrates, proteins, and fats in the normal way. It will also help prevent acute complications—those that occur suddenly and last for a relatively short time—and chronic complications—those that develop slowly and are long-lasting.

What blood sugar range is considered acceptable? Nondiabetic people have blood sugar levels of about 70 to 110 mg/dL before meals, and below about 140 mg/dL a few hours after meals. Target levels for people with diabetes vary from person to person. For some, it is within this range; for others, it is higher.

Good control of blood sugar levels requires balancing food intake, physical exercise, and, in some people, insulin or oral drugs. As Figure 5 shows, food

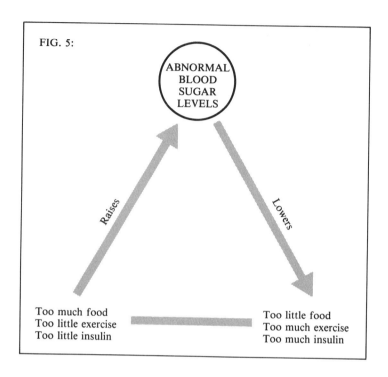

FIG. 5:

ABNORMAL BLOOD SUGAR LEVELS

Raises

Lowers

Too much food
Too little exercise
Too little insulin

Too little food
Too much exercise
Too much insulin

raises blood sugar levels, and exercise and insulin lower blood sugar levels. Too much food, too little exercise, or too little insulin can raise blood sugar levels too high; too little food, too much exercise, or too much insulin can push blood sugar levels too low.

Controlling stress seems to be important in many patients. Common forms of stress include physical stress, such as illness or strenuous exercise; and mental stress, such as worry and anxiety. In what is called the "fight or flight" response, a person or animal faced with danger undergoes rapid physical changes that prepare it to stand and fight vigorously or to run. The heart "pounds," blood pressure rises, the amount of blood flowing to the muscles increases, and the muscles become ready for vigorous action.

Epinephrine and other stress hormones are involved in the "fight or flight" reaction. They put the body's stored energy to work by making sugar and fatty acids available for use. People who do not have diabetes can use the sugar immediately, but those with diabetes may not have enough insulin available to prevent sugar buildup in the blood.

Mike's Treatment Plan

The same afternoon that Michael, the ninth-grader, vomited at school, his doctor sent him to a diabetes clinic at a nearby hospital. Mike was hospitalized for several days while a health-care team started his insulin therapy, taught him how to inject his insulin, and planned his treatment program. The diabetes health-care team was made up of a doctor who specializes in diabetes, a diabetes nurse-educator, a registered dietitian (an expert in nutrition and meal planning), an ophthalmologist (an M.D. who specializes in eye diseases), a podiatrist (a specialist in foot care), an exercise specialist, and a counselor. Mike was very lucky, for such teams are not available to every diabetes patient.

In later visits to the clinic, Mike's team taught him how to adjust his meal plan and insulin schedule so that he could play baseball and go to summer camp. Mike's parents and brother also learned about his treatment, so that they would know what to do in an emergency if Mike's blood sugar levels became too high or too low.

One of the most important things Mike learned at the clinic was how to use blood and urine tests at home. The team told him what types of tests were best for him and when and how to test. They also explained how to adjust his insulin, food intake, and exercise if his blood sugar levels became a little too high or too low. The nurse gave him a special book for recording his test results and any changes in the treatment program, so that he and the team could review them.

Mike learned how to recognize the symptoms that go along with too-high and too-low blood sugar levels. He also found out what to do if he developed a cold or other illness that could change his blood sugar levels. He learned that he must call the clinic right away if his blood sugar levels became very high or very low.

Mr. Gordon's Treatment Plan

Mr. Gordon, the fifty-two-year-old, was shocked when his doctor told him he had diabetes. Immediately he thought about his late father, who had also had Type II and was overweight. His father hadn't paid much attention to his diabetes. After several years he'd died of a heart attack.

Mr. Gordon was determined to do whatever was necessary to get his blood sugar levels down. Unless he did, he would face an above-average risk of heart disease, stroke, and impotence (inability to have an erection of the penis and to complete the sex act).

The doctor told Mr. Gordon that the most important thing was to lose weight. He suggested a diet and exercise program, and explained that if Mr. Gordon would lose about 40 pounds, his body's own insulin would work better. Then his blood sugar levels would probably return to normal. Otherwise, Mr. Gordon would have to take an oral hypoglycemic drug. He might also need insulin injections during times of illness or surgery, and eventually he might even need insulin to live.

After talking with the exercise specialist, Mr. Gordon decided that he would take his dog for a long walk several times a week. He would also get off the train a stop ahead of time every day and use the stairs at work instead of the elevator. Mr. Gordon made an appointment to return to the clinic in four weeks to see how well his weight-loss program was working.

Monitoring Blood Sugar Levels at Home

Like other diabetic patients, Michael and Mr. Gordon were taught to use blood tests at home to check their blood sugar levels. They would use the information from these tests to adjust food intake, insulin dose, and exercise, in order to keep blood sugar levels under control.

A finger-sticking device called a lancet is used to draw a small drop of blood from a fingertip. Although this may sound painful, spring-operated lancets cause little if any discomfort. The drop of blood is placed on a chemically treated test strip. Depending upon the strip used, the drop is blotted, wiped, or washed away after about a minute. In another minute or so the strip develops a color.

The color, which indicates the amount of sugar in the blood, can be read in either of two ways. One way is to compare it with colors on a color chart, usually found on the test-strip container. The matching color indicates a range of blood sugar levels, such as 80 to 120 mg/dL, but does not give a specific number value. Or, the strip can be read by inserting it into a small instrument called a meter. Within a minute or two the meter automatically shows a numerical value, such as 117 mg/dL.

Using Urine Tests to Check Blood Sugar Levels

How can urine tests be used to check the amount of sugar in the blood? Normally, urine contains at most a trace of sugar. You may remember that when blood sugar levels get too high, the kidneys "spill" some sugar into the urine. The blood sugar level at which the kidneys remove excess sugar from the blood is called the renal threshold. It averages about 180 mg/ dL. In other words, when the blood sugar level is higher than about 180 mg/dL, the kidneys usually begin excreting sugar into the urine.

But urine tests for sugar give only a rough idea of sugar levels in the blood. One reason is that the renal threshold varies widely. One person can have a high blood sugar level without spilling sugar into the urine, while another spills sugar even when blood sugar levels are fairly low.

Another problem with urine tests is that they do not detect low blood sugar levels, and this information can be very important.

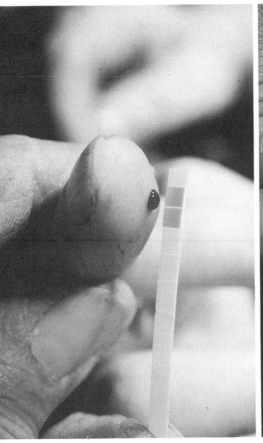
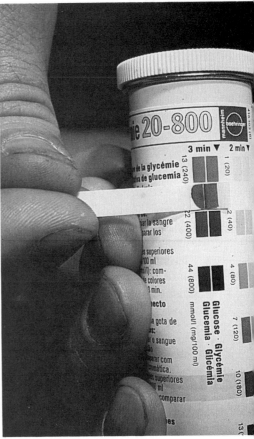

(Left) A blood sample is applied to a chemically treated test strip used to measure sugar levels in the blood.

(Right) The color that develops on the strip is then compared with a color chart that indicates glucose count in the blood. This particular test shows a high level of 280 mg/dL.

A third problem is that the urine sample may have collected in the bladder hours before the test. Urine is produced continually by the kidneys and stored in the bladder until it is released from the body. For this reason, urine tests may indicate high blood sugar levels when blood sugar levels have actually returned to normal (or vice versa). One way to minimize this problem is to test the first and second urine samples in the morning. Obtaining the second morning sample involves emptying the bladder upon arising (the first sample), taking a drink of water, waiting about thirty minutes, then emptying the bladder again. The first sample reflects blood sugar levels over the previous several hours, while the second sample indicates levels closer to the time of testing.

Procedures for measuring sugar in urine are similar to those for measuring sugar in blood. Special tablets or chemically treated papers or sticks are placed in contact with a small amount of urine or urine plus water. The color that develops is compared with colors on a chart to yield the test result.

Urine Tests for Detecting Ketones

Many diabetic people need to test their urine for ketones to make sure that blood sugar levels are within an acceptable range. Testing for ketones is especially important during illness and whenever the blood sugar level is high—generally about 240 mg/dL or above, although the level varies from person to person. Even people with Type II may need to test for ketones during illness and often more frequently.

Urinary ketone test kits use tablets or treated sticks and a color chart. The chart indicates no ketones, a trace of ketones, or a small, moderate, or large amount of ketones. Some ketone kits test urine for sugar as well.

The presence of moderate or large amounts of ketones is a danger signal. It means that blood sugar levels need to be brought under better control. The person needs to call the doctor, take more insulin, or follow other instructions given earlier by the health-care team.

How Often Do People
Test the Blood and Urine?

The health-care team tells the patient when and how often to test, and what tests to use. Testing is especially important during illness and whenever there is a change in diet, activity level, or dose of insulin or drug that affects blood sugar levels, such as an oral hypoglycemic drug.

Blood sugar levels are especially hard to control in certain Type I patients. These people are more likely than others to develop complications, so they may need to test their blood sugar levels four or more times each day. They also need to check often for urinary ketones. Depending on the test results, they may need to adjust their diet, activity level, or insulin dosage and schedule. Although urine tests for sugar cannot be used to adjust the treatment program, some people use them along with blood tests to provide detailed information about blood sugar control.

Blood sugar levels are easier to control in pa-

*A young woman diabetic checks her blood
sugar level with a personal glucometer.*

tients with Type II, so blood and urine tests are usually performed far less often.

Office Visits

Amy visits the diabetes clinic regularly for routine checkups. During these visits, her height and weight are checked to make sure she is growing normally. The areas where she injects insulin are examined, and her legs and feet are inspected for sores, blisters, and other problems. The team also reviews Amy's record book and adjusts the treatment program if necessary.

Other office procedures performed from time to time in patients with diabetes include a complete physical exam, a careful eye exam, and a variety of lab tests, including tests to measure the blood levels of fats and *cholesterol*. If the various procedures show that the patient has problems such as high blood pressure, kidney disease, eye disorders, or abnormal levels of fats or cholesterol in the blood, treatment is started right away. Early treatment can help lower the risk of some of the complications of diabetes.

The Glycosylated Hemoglobin Test

Every few months, many people with diabetes have a special test called the *glycosylated hemoglobin test*. This test, performed in the doctor's office, indicates how well blood sugar levels are controlled over a prolonged period. It does so by measuring the glycosylated hemoglobin level.

How does the test work? Hemoglobin is a pigment that gives red blood cells their color. When blood sugar levels rise, glucose in the blood attaches to hemoglobin in red blood cells. It remains attached for the life of the blood cell, which is about 120 days. The glycosylated hemoglobin test measures the amount of glucose bound to hemoglobin. If the level is high, it means that average blood sugar levels have been on the high side over the past few months.

Long-Term Health Problems

Some people who have had diabetes for many years develop related health problems. Damage to the blood vessels caused by diabetes can interfere with normal blood flow, injuring the body's tissues. This sometimes leads to heart disease, stroke, kidney disease, or blindness. Because cigarette smoking also interferes with blood flow, the risk is much higher in those who smoke.

Nerve damage associated with diabetes can result in impotence and other problems. It can also cause pain, tingling, burning, or loss of feeling in the feet, legs, or hands. When the nerves and blood vessels that supply the feet are damaged, a small blister or cut may go unnoticed and become infected. In severe cases, infection or an inadequate blood supply can result in loss of the foot or leg, but this happens in only a small percentage of diabetic people. Although complications of diabetes are a leading cause of death, many people with diabetes live a normal life-span.

Some complications can be successfully treated, especially if found early. Also, evidence suggests that good control of blood sugar levels can help prevent, lessen, postpone, or perhaps even reverse some of the complications. Thanks to recent medical advances and better medical care, the percentage of people developing serious complications is smaller than it was just a few years ago. Experts say that if a person with diabetes visits the doctor regularly, follows instructions about meals, physical activity, and medication, and does not smoke, he or she should expect to enjoy a relatively normal, productive life.

Coping with Feelings

People who learn that they have diabetes may feel angry, frightened, or confused. Young people who are becoming independent find it especially hard to accept a lifelong disease—one that involves daily treatment and monitoring, changes in life-style, close contact with the health-care team, and help from family members when problems develop. One of the last things young people want is to be different, yet those with diabetes need to follow regular meal times and snack times, while their friends can skip lunch and grab a shake or a soda and fries after school. Those with diabetes also need to have enough sleep and get up at the same time every morning, while their friends can party half the night and sleep late.

Hormonal and physical changes of adolescence make blood sugar levels hard to control. Ups and downs in blood sugar levels can cause mood swings, intensifying the emotional upheavals of adolescence. It's clear that coping with diabetes is especially difficult during this period. Many communities have support groups where young adults with diabetes can talk with each other and work out some of their problems.

Todd, who developed diabetes when he was thirteen, found it especially hard to adjust. He kept thinking how unfair it was. "Why me? Why do I have to be different? I want to be like everyone else."

Because Todd was angry and embarrassed, he refused to go anywhere with his friends. They became angry with him. Then Todd started talking with his doctor, counselor, and best friend. He decided that the best way to avoid being "different" was to try to accept diabetes as just another burden to cope with—along with his acne and his kid brother, who was giving him lots of problems. Once Todd had his insulin and meal schedule under control, he started to think of himself as a regular kid who happened to have diabetes. And once this happened, he found that others didn't think of him as "different" either.

Amy found her family's attitude the hardest thing to cope with. She felt that her mother was constantly watching to make sure she ate the things she was supposed to, while her dad was always nagging her about taking her insulin and doing her blood sugar tests. Amy had started to make good progress with her diabetes, but she was getting so exasperated with her parents that she felt like giving up.

"It's none of their business how often I test!" Amy complained to the nurse at the clinic. "Why are

Thomas Nash, 16, is a Type I diabetic who has handled his own injections since he was 11 years old. An active athlete, Nash was the only freshman on his school's varsity basketball team. "For me," he says, "the hardest part was when I was growing up and I didn't want to tell people about my diabetes because I didn't really accept it myself—and I was afraid they'd think I was different. Now I accept it. And I know that if anything, people will admire what I'm doing."

they always after me? I know what I'm supposed to do. It's my life, not theirs!"

The nurse talked with Amy about her feelings and her parents' attitudes. She suggested that if her mom and dad understood how Amy felt, they might be able to take things more calmly. Amy agreed, so she invited her parents to attend support meetings where parents of adolescents with diabetes talk about their problems. From what they learned at the meetings, Amy's parents began to realize that they were being too protective, and that Amy was taking good care of herself. With the nurse's encouragement, they agreed to help if asked, but otherwise to stay back. Amy, who was attending an adolescent support group, promised that if her parents had questions or concerns she would go over her record book with them once a week. But as time passed, her parents asked less often. One day when Amy came down with the flu she asked her parents for help, and they were careful to do only what was necessary.

CHAPTER

6

MEALS AND SNACKS

Most foods contain a combination of carbohydrates, proteins, and fats. As you've learned, carbohydrates (sugars and starches) are broken down into glucose, providing quick energy. Simple carbohydrates are found in table sugar, honey, candy, syrup, jams, jellies, soda pop, desserts, and similar foods. Complex carbohydrates are contained in bread, pasta, cereal, rice, and starchy vegetables. Fiber is a plant material found in some carbohydrate foods, such as fruits, vegetables, and whole-grain cereals and breads.

Protein is used by the body to repair and maintain tissue and to build new tissue. Proteins of animal origin are found in meat, poultry, fish, milk, cheese, and eggs. Proteins from plants are found in peas, beans, grains, cereals, and nuts.

Fat is used as a source of fatty acid and as a fuel reserve. Fat takes longer to digest than proteins or carbohydrates, giving a feeling of fullness. It contains about twice as many calories per gram as protein or carbohydrate.

Food contains three types of fats: saturated, monounsaturated, and polyunsaturated. Saturated fats are solid at room temperature. They tend to raise the level of cholesterol in the blood. Most saturated fats come from foods of animal origin, such as beef, pork, lamb, cheese, milk, and butter. Palm oil and coconut oil also contain saturated fats.

Monounsaturated and polyunsaturated fats are liquid at room temperature. In moderate amounts they help lower the cholesterol level of the blood. Monounsaturated fats are found in peanut oil and olive oil, and polyunsaturated fats are contained in various vegetable oils, such as corn, cottonseed, sunflower, safflower, and soybean.

Cholesterol is a fatlike substance found only in animal products, especially egg yolks and butter. The body needs some cholesterol, but too much can contribute to the formation of fat deposits in the walls of the arteries. This may block the flow of blood to and from the heart.

An individualized meal plan is developed for the diabetic patient, based on height, weight, activity level, and food preferences. A typical meal plan consists of three meals and several snacks. Appropriate foods are basically the same as those everyone should eat, but simple sugars, fats, and often salt are limited. Mealtimes and the amount and type of food taken at each meal are determined by the person's life-style and activity pattern.

Meal Planning in Type I

The typical American diet is too high in fat and simple carbohydrates. General dietary guidelines for people with Type I are the same as those for anyone who wants to follow healthy eating habits. They include:

•   Eating larger amounts of complex carbohydrates. The American Diabetes Association recommends that people with diabetes obtain slightly more than half of their calories from carbohydrates, especially complex carbohydrates and naturally occurring sugars, such as those in fruit and milk. Simple carbohydrates are limited because they are rapidly absorbed into the bloodstream and can quickly raise blood sugar levels. (Recent studies suggest that some simple sugars do not raise blood sugar levels significantly if eaten with other types of foods, but more information is needed on this subject.) Foods high in fiber help in digestion and seem to help lower blood sugar and blood fat levels.

•   Eating less fat. Most of us should eat less saturated fat and cholesterol, replacing some of it with monounsaturated and polyunsaturated fats. It's generally recommended that less than 30 percent of our daily calories come from fat and 20 percent or less from protein. Cholesterol intake should be less than 300 mg daily.

•   Using less salt. Eating a lot of salt can sometimes lead to high blood pressure. This, in turn, raises the risk of heart and blood-vessel disease.

•   Using alcohol in moderation, if at all. As will be discussed in Chapter Ten, drinking alcoholic beverages can make it much more difficult to control blood sugar levels.

In Type I diabetes, the amount of carbohydrate, protein, and fat eaten should be about the same from day to day. Although intake of simple carbohydrates is limited, ice cream, cake, and other sweets can be included on special occasions. And delicious desserts can be prepared with artificial (nonsugar) sweeteners.

To help with meal planning in Type I, the American Diabetes Association and the American Dietetic Association have organized the six basic food groups into Exchange Lists. The six Exchange Lists are:

1. Starches and breads
2. Meat, fish, poultry, cheeses, and other protein-rich foods
3. Vegetables
4. Fruits
5. Milk
6. Fats

Each serving within an Exchange List contains approximately the same amount of carbohydrate, protein, fat, and calories.

The lists are easy to follow. For example, 1 milk exchange is 1 8-ounce glass of skim milk, 1 bread exchange is 1 slice of bread, and 1 fruit is a small orange. Food should be weighed or measured until the person learns how to estimate amounts.

Any food in an Exchange List can be traded (exchanged) for another in that list. For example, Tommy hates fish, so he "trades" it, ounce for ounce, for lean beef. Susie can't stand squash; instead she eats corn on the cob.

Casseroles and other dishes contain foods that fit into several Exchange Lists. For example, the exchanges in one-fourth of a typical 10-inch thin-crust cheese pizza are 2 starch, 2 medium-fat meat, and 1 fat. Exchanges in an 8-ounce can (1 cup) of spaghetti and meatballs are 2 starch, 1 medium-fat meat, and 1 fat. Dietitians can provide information about the patient's favorite foods, and the American Diabetes Association and American Dietetic Association publish cookbooks that contain tasty recipes with information about nutrient content.

Some studies suggest that cooking procedures, the content of the meal, and other factors may change the effect of carbohydrates on blood sugar levels. It seems that under certain conditions, some simple carbohydrates may raise blood sugar levels less than some complex carbohydrates (starches) do. When more information becomes available, perhaps meal plans will be changed to include the glycemic index, which is a scale that measures the ability of various foods to raise blood sugar levels over a period of time.

The meal plan developed for each Type I patient lists total calories; grams and percentages of carbohydrate, protein, and fat; mealtimes and snack times; and the number of exchanges. The same basic menu can be used for the entire family, with family members adding or substituting foods as desired. In fact, when someone develops diabetes, often other family members benefit from healthier eating habits.

Meals and snacks should be eaten at specific times throughout the day so that food intake is balanced with insulin levels and physical activity. People who do not have diabetes produce greater or lesser amounts of insulin to match the amount of food eaten. People with diabetes have to match their food intake with the amount of insulin injected.

The meal plan provides some flexibility. What if Susie's having dinner at a friend's house and doesn't know what time dinner will be served? Simple. She can eat a bagel before leaving home and skip her bread exchange at dinner.

Meal Planning in Type II

Because most people with Type II are overweight, the basic goal is to reach and maintain normal weight. This usually allows the body to use its own insulin. The diet limits calories, and an exercise program is included to help in weight loss.

Eating less may sharply lower the blood sugar level even before a lot of weight is lost. Most people who reach their ideal weight can keep their blood sugar levels within normal range without the help of drugs.

But if they gain back the extra weight, blood sugar levels rise again.

People who are not obese when they develop Type II follow the same meal-planning guidelines as people with Type I. Some also need oral drugs or insulin to control symptoms.

CHAPTER

7

SPORTS AND
EXERCISE

Exercise is good for almost everyone. It helps in weight loss, reduces tension, and improves the feeling of well-being. Because it helps lower the blood pressure and the amount of fat in the blood, it also helps protect against heart and blood-vessel disease. In Type I exercise boosts the blood-sugar-lowering effect of injected insulin, and in Type II it helps lower insulin resistance.

Exercise also lowers blood sugar levels by helping cells use glucose more quickly. In fact, children with severe diabetes who lead a very active life need less insulin than they would otherwise. Why is this?

Most of the time muscle cells obtain energy from fatty acids rather than glucose. But in two situations, muscles use large amounts of glucose. One is during strenuous exercise. During these periods, for reasons not clearly understood, large amounts of insulin are not necessary to allow glucose to enter the muscle cells. The second situation is during the few hours after a meal, when blood sugar levels are high and the pancreas produces large amounts of insulin. The extra insulin moves sugar rapidly into muscle cells, which use the sugar instead of fatty acids for energy.

Activities especially helpful for diabetic patients include bicycling, swimming, skating, cross-country skiing, running, and vigorous walking. These activities, called aerobic sports, involve continuous, repetitive use of large muscles. They increase the body's use of oxygen to meet energy needs. When aerobic sports are performed for at least twenty minutes several times a week, they improve the function of the circulatory and respiratory systems, help in weight loss, and help lower blood sugar levels.

Anaerobic sports, such as tennis and golf, are stop-and-start activities. They involve short bursts of activity rather than continuous vigorous movement. Although anaerobic sports can help in weight loss,

Chantre Randolph was 8 years old when she was diagnosed a diabetic. Whenever she tests her blood and finds that her sugar level is up, she jumps rope or dances, and keeps active.

lowering of blood sugar levels, and tension reduction, and can be a lot of fun, they do not improve cardio-vascular and respiratory fitness.

Exercise and Type I

The exercise program is started once blood sugar levels are under control. Exercise periods are usually planned for after a meal, when blood sugar levels are rising. Exercise should be avoided when insulin levels are low or at their highest, unless food intake is adjusted.

Ideally, people with Type I should have the same amount of exercise each day, at about the same time. A change in the amount or time changes the need for food, insulin, or both. Because people react differently to exercise, the only way to find out exactly how much food someone needs is by testing blood sugar levels before, during, and after exercise. The health-care team reviews the test results and adjusts the meal and insulin schedule if necessary.

Suppose Kevin decides to go for a swim or bike ride on the spur of the moment. He needs to eat a high-protein snack first, such as cheese or a meat sandwich. This will help avoid an *insulin reaction,* in which insulin levels get too high and drive blood sugar levels too low. Insulin reactions cause trembling, sweating, and confusion. When a reaction sets in, fruit juice, sugar cubes, raisins, or other simple sugars will quickly raise the blood sugar.

A full day of strenuous activity can be planned with the help of the health-care team. When Kevin decided to go on an all-day skiing trip, his health-care team told him how to adjust his meals and insulin dose. As always, he carried raisins and sugar cubes in his pocket. He also told the guide about his diabetes, so that she would know what to do if he needed help.

Exercise and Type II

Lenora recently learned that she has Type II diabetes. She decided to try to lower her blood sugar levels through exercise and a weight-loss diet rather than by taking oral drugs. Her doctor suggested brisk walking, but cautioned that she should begin slowly. During the first week, she was to walk slowly for five minutes (the warm-up period), then briskly for five minutes, then slowly again for five minutes (the cooldown period). She was to do this at least three times a week. Over three to six months she could gradually increase the walking time to about forty minutes. She could then take up swimming, bicycle riding, or another sport if she wanted to.

The program worked well. In fact, a friend who wanted to lose weight decided to go with her, and the two enjoyed their walks together. After a few months they had lost some weight and felt good about themselves. Lenora was especially happy that she could control her blood sugar levels without taking drugs.

CHAPTER

8

INSULIN AND ORAL HYPOGLYCEMIC DRUGS

Fortunately, the days of rancid old meats, blood and suet pudding, and starvation diets are long gone. Today's patients have modern drugs to help control their diabetes—insulin for Type I patients and oral hypoglycemic agents for Type II patients who need drug therapy.

Types of Insulin

When insulin first became available in 1922, it was so short-acting that patients needed three to six injections a day. Many patients today need just one or two shots daily.

Three major types of insulin are available: regular, or short-acting (also called rapid-acting), intermediate-acting, and long-acting. The three types differ in how soon they reach the bloodstream and start working (onset), how long they act (duration of action), and when their action is the strongest (peak). The exact onset, duration, and peak of action also vary from person to person, and in a given person from day to day.

Regular, or *short-acting, insulin* starts working in about thirty minutes, peaks about one-half to two hours after injection, and stays in the bloodstream for eight to twelve hours. This type of insulin is clear (transparent). A special type of regular insulin, called Semilente, acts a little more slowly. It starts working in one to two hours and peaks in three to eight hours.

Intermediate-acting insulin starts working in about two to four hours, peaks about eight to twelve hours after injection, and remains in the bloodstream for eighteen to twenty-six hours. Intermediate-acting (and long-acting) insulin is not as clear as regular insulin because ingredients have been added to delay the insulin's release. The two varieties of intermediate-acting insulin are Lente and NPH.

Long-acting insulin begins working in six to eight hours, peaks in fourteen to twenty-four hours, and stays in the bloodstream for up to thirty-six hours. The two varieties of long-acting insulin are Ultralente and PZI.

Insulin is available in several concentrations. The higher the concentration, the smaller the amount to be injected. The most widely used is the highest strength, called U-100.

Sources of Insulin

Insulin obtained from pigs and cows has been used for many years, and some preparations contain a mixture of the two types. Human insulin became available more recently. Some brands of human insulin are made by chemically changing pork insulin, while others are produced by changing bacteria through genetic engineering. Figure 6 is a simplified illustration of the process involved in mass-producing human insulin. Both types of human insulin are chemically the same as insulin produced by the normal human pancreas. Highly purified pork insulins and especially the two types of human insulin seem to cause fewer allergic reactions than other types.

Insulin Administration and Schedules

The goal in insulin therapy is to provide a continuous low level of insulin throughout the day and night, with larger amounts at mealtimes. Insulin will then be available when food is being digested and glucose enters the blood.

The insulin schedule is planned individually. It is adjusted for children as they grow, and for all patients during illness and as activity levels change. The type of insulin used may be changed from time to time to provide better control.

Many patients receive two injections daily, given about thirty minutes before a meal. Each injection combines short-acting and intermediate-acting insulin. As the effect of the short-acting type diminishes, the intermediate-acting begins to work. Other people do best with three injections; short- and intermediate-acting insulin at breakfast, short-acting at dinner, and intermediate-acting at bedtime. People who take two

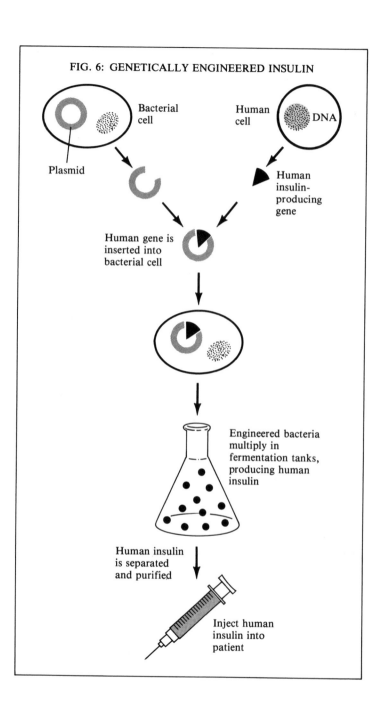

FIG. 6: GENETICALLY ENGINEERED INSULIN

Bacterial cell

Human cell

DNA

Plasmid

Human insulin-producing gene

Human gene is inserted into bacterial cell

Engineered bacteria multiply in fermentation tanks, producing human insulin

Human insulin is separated and purified

Inject human insulin into patient

different kinds of insulin at once, such as short- and intermediate-acting, are taught how to draw both types into one syringe and inject them together.

Insulin is usually provided in a bottle and drawn up into a needle for injection. Among other delivery systems are pen-size cartridges that contain enough insulin for several injections.

Intensive Insulin Therapy

In diabetes that is difficult to control, called brittle or labile diabetes, blood sugar levels can quickly shift between very high and very low. Four or more insulin injections may be needed each day to mimic the way a healthy pancreas delivers insulin. Blood sugar levels are monitored frequently so insulin dosage and timing can be adjusted to provide better control.

Another way sometimes used to provide "tight" control is to give insulin through a pumping device worn on a belt. The device, about the size of a deck of cards, consists of a microprocessor and a small syringe filled with insulin. The computer is programmed to deliver a specific amount of insulin over twenty-four hours. Insulin is delivered in continuous "drips" through a small tube attached to a needle that is inserted through the skin, usually in the abdomen. Mealtimes can be more flexible than before, because the patient pushes a button shortly before a meal to deliver a larger amount of insulin. Every one to three days the insulin container inside the pump is refilled, tubing and needle are replaced, and the injection site is changed.

An insulin pump can be extremely useful for people who cannot control their blood sugar levels satisfactorily despite multiple daily insulin injections and close monitoring. Pregnant women and others for whom tight control is especially important may also find the pump helpful.

People have to be highly motivated to use a pump successfully. Diet, exercise, monitoring, and record-keeping are just as important as ever, and it's important to have twenty-four-hour access to a physician or other health-care professional trained in pump use.

Injection Sites

Sites for injecting insulin include various areas of fatty tissue—the front of the thigh; the upper area of the buttocks, behind the hip bone; the outer area of the upper arm; and the abdomen, just above and below the waist (but not within a 2-inch circle around the navel). Some areas are hard to reach, but family members can help by injecting these areas.

The injection site is rotated (changed) regularly to help prevent small dents and lumps from forming in the skin. For example, the upper arm is used for several days or a few weeks, depending on the person's size and the number of injections given each day. When available spaces in the upper arm have been used, injections are made in another area. The sites used are recorded.

The site of injection affects how quickly insulin is absorbed into the blood. Exercising the muscles in a given area increases blood flow to that area and

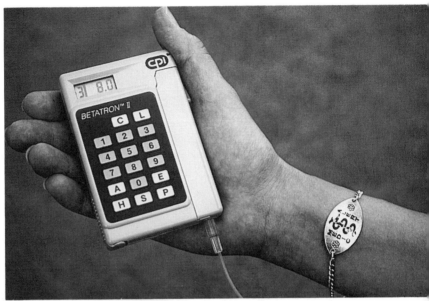

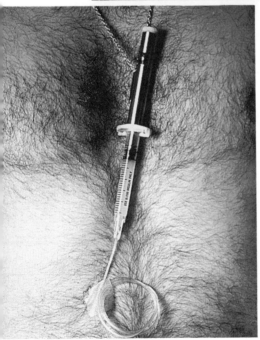

(Above) An automatic insulin pump rests in a diabetic's hand. In an emergency, the bracelet alerts medics that the patient is diabetic and may be insulin-dependent. (Left) This syringe driver delivers insulin to a person with diabetes. When the top can is turned, a measured dose of insulin is pumped from the syringe into the needle, which is embedded under the skin.

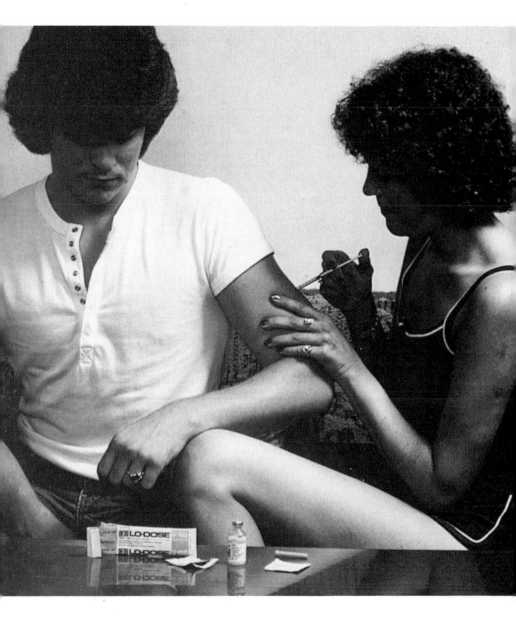

*An adult injects insulin
into a diabetic.*

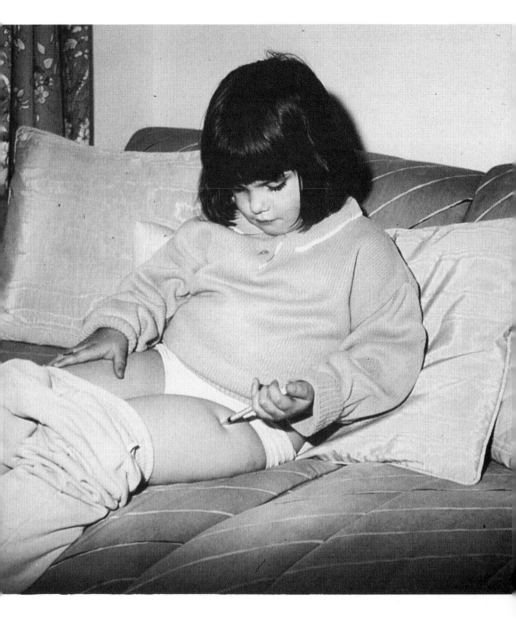

*A five-year-old diabetic child
injects herself with insulin.*

speeds the rate of absorption. This can cause an un-expected lowering of blood sugar. For this reason, people should avoid injecting insulin into an area that will soon be exercised. A leg site shouldn't be used just before a bike ride, and a site in the arm or leg shouldn't be used before a swim.

Oral Hypoglycemic Drugs

Oral hypoglycemic drugs do not contain insulin, contrary to what some people believe. Insulin is a protein. If taken by mouth, it would be destroyed by the enzymes that help digest food.

Doctors aren't certain exactly how oral hypoglycemic drugs work. Some seem to make the body cells more sensitive to insulin, while others appear to stimulate the pancreas to produce more insulin.

Oral drugs are useless in people with Type I. They help only when the body can produce some insulin. Moreover, oral drugs are effective only if the person follows the doctor's instructions about diet, exercise, and weight loss. They do not work at all in some Type II people, and in others they stop working after several months or years.

Oral hypoglycemic drugs are taken once, twice, or three times a day and act for varying lengths of time. Many Type II people who lose weight and keep it off no longer need pills.

CHAPTER

DIABETIC EMERGENCIES

In Type I diabetes, potentially serious reactions may develop when blood sugar levels become too low or too high. Most reactions can be treated by the patient or the family, and almost always the person recovers fully. Acute reactions are rare in Type II.

Low Blood Sugar Levels (Hypoglycemia) and Insulin Reactions

An insulin reaction can develop when blood sugar levels fall below about 50 mg/dL. An abnormally low blood sugar level is called *hypoglycemia*. The cause of the drop in blood sugar levels may be too much insulin, too little food, a delayed mealtime, too much exercise, illness, alcohol taken on an empty stomach, or a combination of these factors. The reaction comes on very quickly, usually just before mealtime or during strenuous activity.

This was what happened late one afternoon when nine-year-old Jackie went to her friend Melissa's house. The girls had planned to work on a math assignment, but Melissa's dog, Champ, was looking for some fun. Barking loudly and wagging his tail, he dropped a tennis ball at Jackie's feet and dashed to the door. The girls laughed, tossed their books aside, and ran outside to play with Champ.

After Jackie played for a while, she started feeling silly. She began running in circles and laughing hysterically. Suddenly she felt nervous and shaky. Her head hurt and she broke into a sweat. Jackie shouted something, but Melissa couldn't understand what she was saying. Jackie was trying to ask Melissa for the sugar cubes in her purse inside the house.

Melissa's mother heard Jackie yelling and hurried into the yard. She saw that Jackie was pale, confused, and breathing heavily. She knew that Jackie had diabetes, so she quickly gave her a small glass of orange juice and told her to sit down. In a few minutes Jackie felt better and asked for a cheese sandwich and some milk. After she'd recovered, she vowed that next time she'd remember to have a snack before playing.

Jackie's problem was an insulin reaction. Because she hadn't taken a snack before running and playing close to dinnertime, her blood sugar level had dropped too low.

Insulin reactions can almost always be controlled

by taking a small amount of raisins, sugar cubes, fruit juice, hard candy, or other food that will quickly raise the blood sugar level. Rarely, a severe reaction develops in which the person loses consciousness. Jackie's parents keep an emergency kit in the refrigerator at home in case this happens. The kit contains glucagon, the pancreatic hormone that has the opposite effect of insulin. Jackie's parents have been taught how to inject glucagon to raise her blood sugar levels very quickly if she loses consciousness. If glucagon is not available, a person having a severe insulin reaction must be rushed to the nearest hospital for treatment.

People with Type II who take oral drugs can develop hypoglycemic reactions, but this is rare. When it happens it is usually caused by skipping a meal or taking too high a dose of the drug.

High Blood Sugar Levels and Ketoacidosis (Diabetic Coma)

When blood sugar levels become too high, ketoacidosis, or diabetic coma, can result. The usual causes are illness or infection, too little insulin, overeating, or a combination of these factors. Unable to use glucose for energy, the body burns fats and proteins instead. Eventually ketones build up in the blood and spill into the urine. The body helps rid itself of one type of ketone, called acetone, through the lungs, giving the breath a sweetish, fruity odor. Other symptoms brought on by an insulin reaction and ketoacidosis are listed in Figure 7.

Usually it takes several days for ketoacidosis to

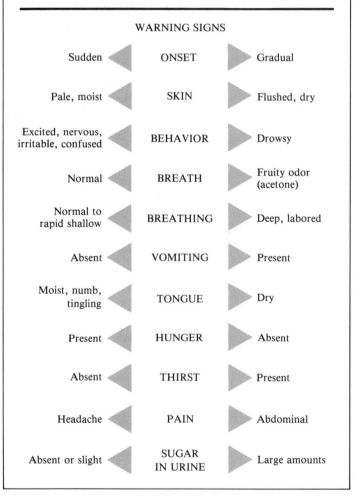

FIG. 7: WARNING SIGNS IN INSULIN REACTION
AND KETOACIDOSIS

HYPOGLYCEMIC
REACTION
(Insulin Reaction)

KETOACIDOSIS
(Diabetic Coma)

WARNING SIGNS

HYPOGLYCEMIC REACTION	WARNING SIGN	KETOACIDOSIS
Sudden	ONSET	Gradual
Pale, moist	SKIN	Flushed, dry
Excited, nervous, irritable, confused	BEHAVIOR	Drowsy
Normal	BREATH	Fruity odor (acetone)
Normal to rapid shallow	BREATHING	Deep, labored
Absent	VOMITING	Present
Moist, numb, tingling	TONGUE	Dry
Present	HUNGER	Absent
Absent	THIRST	Present
Headache	PAIN	Abdominal
Absent or slight	SUGAR IN URINE	Large amounts

develop. Fortunately, the problem is almost always detected before it becomes serious. People who monitor their blood sugar levels and urinary ketones can see trouble developing and take steps to lower their blood sugar levels.

When Amy noticed that her blood sugar levels had been rising slowly for several days, she tested her urine and found a moderate amount of ketones. Looking back, she realized that she'd cut back on gymnastics because she'd been studying for finals. This probably had caused her blood sugar levels to rise. She called her doctor and followed instructions for increasing her insulin dose temporarily. Her blood sugar levels soon returned to normal.

But ketoacidosis can also be the first sign of Type I diabetes. When this happens, blood sugar levels can become dangerously high before anyone realizes something is wrong. It's easy to see why someone who feels sleepy, vomits, and has abdominal pain may think it's just a bad case of the flu. But soon the breathing becomes labored, the breath develops a sweet, fruitlike odor, and a coma may develop. The person needs immediate emergency treatment at a hospital.

Ketoacidosis is rare in Type II diabetes. When it does occur, it's usually during illness or stress, especially in older people who live alone.

CHAPTER

10

SELF-CARE

As part of the treatment program, the health-care team provides detailed instructions on care of the feet, skin, teeth, and gums, and gives advice on many other aspects of personal care. But it is the patient who has the primary responsibility for making the treatment program work. He or she is the most important member of the health-care team.

Foot Care

When you cut your foot or develop a blister, it hurts. But because of nerve damage and reduced blood flow to the feet, someone with diabetes may not feel discomfort from cuts, blisters, and other foot problems. Serious infections can result, and hospitalization may be needed. If gangrene (tissue death) occurs, it may be necessary to remove part of the foot or leg. Fortunately, this is now rare.

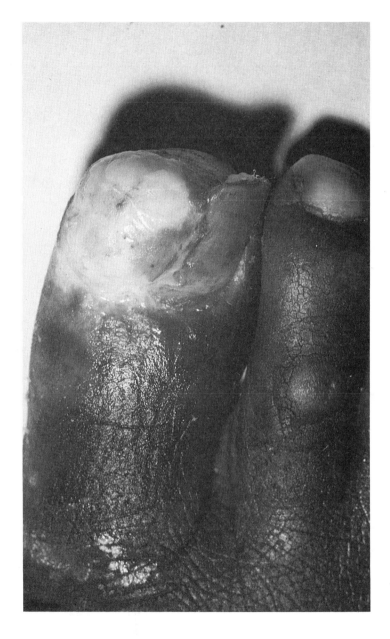

*An example of advanced gangrene of the toes,
a condition caused by diabetes.*

Most foot problems can be prevented by carefully following the health-care team's instructions and having regular foot examinations. Helpful steps include washing (in lukewarm water), carefully drying, and examining the feet daily, and seeking immediate treatment for cuts, sores, blisters, corns, and athlete's foot. Feet need protection from cuts, irritations, and temperature extremes. Shoes that fit well and feel comfortable prevent many problems, and should always be worn when the person is outdoors. Toenails should be cut or filed straight across, level with the top of the toe. Activities that restrict blood flow to the feet must be avoided.

Skin Care

Poorly controlled diabetes can lead to skin infections and other skin problems. Cuts should be washed with soap and water, then observed for warmth, swelling, or redness, which can indicate infection. Any infection, especially one on the hand or foot, needs immediate treatment.

Care of the Teeth and Gums

Problems with the teeth and gums may develop, especially if blood sugar levels are poorly controlled. A special concern is periodontal disease, a condition that can eventually destroy the gums and the bones that support the teeth. Unless periodontal disease is successfully treated, the teeth may become loose and fall out. Visiting the dentist regularly and following instructions about brushing and flossing can help prevent or reverse periodontal disease.

Driving

People with diabetes can drive a car if legally qualified to do so. But they need to take great care to avoid low levels of blood sugar. No diabetic should drive unless blood sugar levels are under good control.

Preparing for Emergencies

Supplies such as hard candies, sugar cubes, and glucose tablets should be on hand to help prevent insulin reactions. When strenuous activity is planned, or if there's a chance that mealtime may be delayed, carrying a form of protein such as crackers and cheese, peanut butter, or a sandwich is always a good idea.

Extra money tucked away in the wallet will pay for a cab to the clinic or hospital in an emergency.

Type I patients should keep a supply of glucagon at home, and family members should be taught how to inject it in case an insulin reaction causes unconsciousness.

Identification

Everyone who takes insulin or an oral hypoglycemic agent should wear a medical ID bracelet or necklace and carry a card identifying them as a diabetic patient. The ID should indicate the person's name, address, telephone number, and type of treatment used.

During Illness

During even a minor illness, blood sugar levels may become difficult to control and insulin needs may rise. The meal plan should be followed as closely as possible. Those who take insulin or an oral hypoglycemic drug should continue to do so, even if they cannot eat. Blood and urine tests are especially important during illness, and the health-care team's instructions must be followed carefully.

Use of Alcohol

Alcohol can increase or decrease the appetite, interfering with the meal schedule. It also tends to affect judgment, which makes it harder to control eating and, consequently, blood sugar levels. When someone drinks alcohol with a sugary mix and eats extra food, blood glucose levels rise. When alcohol is taken without a sugary mix and on an empty stomach, blood sugar levels can drop.

People who drink and become less in touch with what is happening may neglect their monitoring tests. Blood sugar levels may become too high or too low while symptoms go unnoticed. If someone with an alcoholic odor on the breath has an insulin reaction or develops dangerously high blood sugar levels, bystanders and health-care workers may not realize that immediate treatment is needed.

Before deciding whether or not to use alcohol, people with diabetes need to consider these factors and discuss them with the health-care team. Some people will be advised not to drink at all. Those who have an option and decide to drink should do so only occasionally, and only when blood sugar levels are under control. They should never drink on an empty stomach.

Cigarette Smoking

Smoking narrows the blood vessels, interfering with blood flow and causing circulatory problems. This raises the risk of heart attack, stroke, and damage to the eyes, kidneys, nerves, and feet. For health reasons, no one should smoke—and this is especially important in diabetes.

Prescription and Over-the-Counter Drugs

Many prescription and nonprescription drugs raise blood sugar levels, and some interact with oral hypoglycemic agents. Many problems can be avoided by reading the label and checking with the pharmacist or health-care team before taking drugs.

Street Drugs

Marijuana and other street drugs are especially risky for those with diabetes. Like alcoholic beverages, street drugs tend to affect the appetite, reduce awareness of what is happening, and make it more difficult to control blood sugar levels. Street drugs may cause an insulin reaction or raise blood sugar levels to dangerously high levels.

CHAPTER

11

LIVING WITH DIABETES

Perhaps you've wondered if having diabetes severely limits what a person can do in life. Fortunately, people with diabetes can do just about anything anyone else with the same abilities and desires can do. A challenging career, family life, even world-class sports competition—all are within reach.

Careers

Almost all jobs are open to people with diabetes, but some are more suitable than others. Jobs with erratic hours may not be ideal choices, but people who are highly motivated may be willing to adjust to the schedule.

A few careers are closed to insulin-dependent people. People with Type I are barred by law from entering the armed forces, getting a pilot's license, and driving trucks or other commercial vehicles engaged in interstate or foreign commerce. Jobs that entail some risk and require alertness, such as working with machinery, are not prohibited by law, but anyone venturing into such work would need to keep blood sugar levels under excellent control and would have to take great care to prevent insulin reactions.

Marriage and
Family Life

Before a diabetic person marries, it's important that the prospective partner understand all aspects of the disease and the problems that may develop. Couples interested in having children need to discuss the situation with each other and the health-care team. The hereditary risk is minor in Type I, and although it is high in Type II, the disease can almost always be prevented.

In women with Type I, pregnancy requires careful planning, extra effort and expense, and the strong support of the woman's husband and doctor. The problems and stresses are greater than those other women face. But if the pregnancy is closely monitored and the health-care team is experienced in caring for pregnant diabetic patients, chances of a successful outcome for mother and child are almost as high as in women who are not diabetic.

Physical Achievement

Many people with diabetes reach levels of physical prowess that are impressive by any standards. Their

*Renowned Brooklyn Dodger Jackie Robinson
slides into base during a 1947 game.
Although Robinson had diabetes, it didn't
stop him from becoming the first black
player ever to play in the World Series.*

inspiring stories are told in *Diabetes Forecast,* published by the American Diabetes Association, and *Countdown,* a publication of the Juvenile Diabetes Foundation International/The Diabetes Research Foundation.

Among the stories is that of Andrew Field, who fulfilled a dream by hiking across the Pacific Crest Trail. Andrew's six-month, 2,550-mile solo trek took him from Mexico to Canada, across the Mojave Desert and the Sierra and Cascade mountain ranges—a grueling trip that has sometimes taken the lives of other adventurers.

Choosing a different challenge, hiker Kim Hunter walked cross-country from California to Washington, D.C., in the Great Peace March for Global Nuclear Disarmament. Her 3,700-mile trip which led her across the Mojave Desert and the Rocky Mountains, took 260 days to complete.

Many sports figures, past and present, have been highly successful despite diabetes. Take baseball greats Jackie Robinson, Ron Santo, and Catfish Hunter; hockey stars Bobby Clarke and Curt Fraser; professional squash player Ned Edwards; triathletes Bill Carlson and Elizabeth Toumajian; marathon runner Charlie Clark; long-distance bike racer Corbin Mills; and Davis Cup champion and tennis Hall-of-Famer William Talbert. Skydiver Michael Treacy has hundreds of jumps to his credit, plunging from heights upwards of 12,000 feet. Gymnast Andrea White, known to her coaches as "Awesome Andee," developed Type I at the age of ten and trained for the Olympics one year later. The success of these talented athletes is an inspiration to us all.

CHAPTER

12

THE FUTURE

For some reason, Type I and Type II diabetes are becoming increasingly common. In fact, the incidence of Type I is rising so quickly that it is expected to double in some countries in twenty to thirty years. This rapid change suggests that environmental factors may be responsible for the increase.

Type II is also on the rise. More people are living past the age of forty, when they are more likely to get the disease. People also eat more and are less active than in past years. The American Diabetes Association estimates that one out of five Americans born today and living to the age of seventy will develop diabetes—unless scientists find a way to prevent or cure the disease.

Is this likely?

Long-term prospects look good. The American Diabetes Association, Juvenile Diabetes Foundation,

(105)

U.S. government, and other organizations here and abroad are working hard to make this happen. Research programs supported by these groups are making excellent progress in learning about the causes and possible prevention or cure of diabetes. In the meantime, scientists all over the world are working on new ways to treat, prevent, or delay the long-term complications of diabetes.

New Ways to Administer Insulin

One day, people may be able to take insulin without injecting it under the skin. Scientists are using a new technology to develop ways to promote the rapid absorption of insulin into the bloodstream from other routes. Among the possibilities being pursued are inhaling insulin through the nose and giving it in the form of eye drops.

Implantable Insulin Pumps

An implantable insulin packet tucked under the skin of the abdomen is being tested in a number of patients. The packet consists of a miniature pump and a tiny, radio-controlled computer that delivers a small, steady amount of highly concentrated insulin day and night. Before eating or exercising, the patient adjusts the insulin dose by "beaming" a signal from outside the body. The insulin reservoir in the pump is refilled from the outside about every two months.

An even more sophisticated portable device is under development, but its practical use is farther in the future. This device, sometimes called a "closed-loop feedback device" or an "artificial beta cell," is similar to the packet described above, but it also contains a sensor. The sensor monitors the blood sugar level and relays this information to a computer, which uses the information to adjust the amount of insulin released. This means that blood sugar levels can be monitored and closely controlled from inside the body, without the patient's help. Large machines based on this technology are currently in bedside use for a few patients. A small system that can be implanted is the dream of many researchers.

Transplants

One way to provide the right amount of insulin exactly when needed is to transplant a normal pancreas, or part of a pancreas, from a human donor to a diabetic person. Already this has been done in many hundreds of patients. Results have been good over a several-year span, but so far the effect has been temporary. Another "natural" way to provide insulin is to transplant islet cells from human or animal donors. This is being done experimentally.

Whether the transplant is a pancreas or islet cells, the patient needs long-term treatment with immuno-suppressive drugs. These drugs stifle the body's normal rejection response to foreign antigens so that the immune system will accept the transplant instead of destroying it.

Unfortunately, some immunosuppressive drugs block the body's ability to fight infection. Immuno-suppressive drugs also have other side effects. For this reason, transplants are usually performed only in patients who need immunosuppression for other reasons, such as for a kidney transplant, or in patients suffering from serious complications of diabetes. This may change when safer immunosuppressive drugs become available, or when doctors can find another way to protect transplanted organs from the immune system.

Progress in
Treating Eye Disease

Over many years, eye damage leads to blindness in a small percentage of diabetic patients. Fortunately, eye surgeons successfully treat many eye problems by using lasers, which are devices that intensify and sharply focus high-energy light beams. In a procedure called photocoagulation, light beams are aimed at the abnormal areas of the eye to seal bleeding vessels and to halt the disease process. A newer surgical procedure, called vitrectomy, is saving the sight of many people with advanced eye disease. In this procedure, surgeons use special instruments to remove blood and scar tissue from the eye.

Tight Control

Evidence suggests that many long-term complications of diabetes are related to poor control of blood sugar levels. A ten-year study is being conducted by the National Institutes of Health to compare the results of tight and standard control in 1,400 volunteers. In this study, known as The Diabetes Control and Complications Trial, "tight control" means intensive insulin therapy—three or four daily injections or use of the insulin pump, with frequent blood sugar monitoring and adjustment of the insulin dose. "Standard control" means one or two shots daily. If the trial shows that tight control does help prevent or postpone complications of diabetes, patients and health-care teams will work even harder to keep blood sugar levels within near-normal range.

Early Clues for
Predicting Type I

The Juvenile Diabetes Foundation and the National Disease Research Interchange have begun a program to track the cause and progression of diabetes. The program, which involves a large number of patients and their families, is called the Human Biological Data Interchange. Family histories are being used to study environmental triggers and the various genes believed to be linked with diabetes. The information gathered will be used in a computer data base. This should be tremendously helpful to scientists looking for a way to stop diabetes before it develops.

Thousands of schoolchildren serving as volunteers have helped scientists develop screening tests for antibodies that destroy the beta cells. Using these screening tests, doctors have been able to identify susceptible children long before the beta cells were destroyed and the children developed diabetes. The presence of one or more of these antibodies, or mark-

ers—islet cell antibodies (ICA), insulin autoantibodies (IAA), and antibodies against a specific protein of the islet cells (64K antibodies)—can provide doctors with important information, such as how rapidly diabetes is likely to develop.

At present the screening tests are complex and too costly for widespread use. But once they become practical and affordable, it may be possible to prevent Type I by starting therapy as soon as antibodies appear, long before symptoms arise. Already a study is under way to see if a single low-dose insulin injection each day will prevent the disease. Other possibilities include developing a drug to destroy the antibodies that attack the beta cells, or using immunosuppressive drugs to protect the beta cells from destruction.

Gene Manipulation

One of the most exciting possibilities for preventing or curing diabetes involves changing a person's genes.

Actress Mary Tyler Moore requests funds for research into juvenile diabetes before a House Appropriations subcommittee. Moore, a diabetic, is the international chairperson of the Juvenile Diabetes Foundation.

The idea is to prevent the immune system from making antibodies that destroy the beta cells. Already scientists have mastered the basic techniques for changing and replacing genes, and have even transplanted a bacterial gene experimentally into cancer patients. One day it may be possible to replace defective genes—such as those involved in diabetes—with normal genes.

How might this happen? In 1989, researchers at the National Institutes of Health launched a monumental study that will take about fifteen years and cost about three billion dollars. The study, which will involve hundreds of researchers, is known as the Human Genome Project. The goal is to map the *human genome.*

What is the human genome? It's the complete set of instructions for creating a human being. In other words, it's the information contained in the *DNA (deoxyribonucleic acid)* in the chromosomes of each of the body cells (see Figure 8).

DNA carries the hereditary blueprint in units called genes. Each gene encodes (directs the formation of) a single protein, such as insulin. Already thousands of genes have been identified. Among them are genes that encode the HLA antigens, carried on chromosome 6; and the human insulin gene, located on chromosome 11. It's believed that chromosome 11 also contains a linkage marker for Type II. Perhaps other markers linked with diabetes will be found.

Once the human genome has been decoded, scientists will be able to predict much more closely the likelihood that someone will develop diabetes and other diseases. Even more important, they may be able to

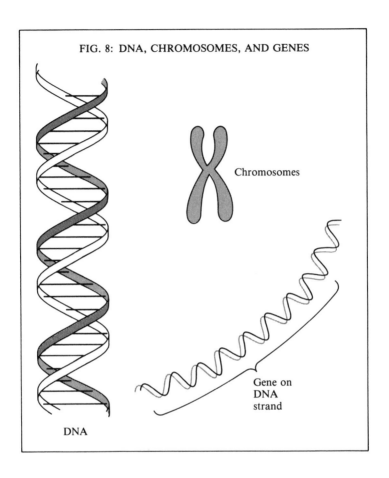

FIG. 8: DNA, CHROMOSOMES, AND GENES

Chromosomes

Gene on
DNA
strand

DNA

prevent such diseases by changing the instructions in
the human genome.

One way to do this would be to take a gene from
a healthy human cell and insert it into the genes of a
harmless virus. The virus would then be allowed to
infect a defective cell from a patient. The virus would
do this by inserting its own DNA, including the normal gene, into the patient's cell. "Recoded" cells

containing the desired instructions would then be injected back into the patient, correcting the genetic defect. If this can be done, and many scientists believe it can, it may be possible one day to prevent diabetes and many other hereditary diseases.

GLOSSARY

Alpha cells: the cells in the islets of Langerhans that make glucagon.

Antibodies: substances the body makes that react with specific antigens invading the body or formed within the body. Antibodies are released into the bloodstream and signal the body's defense system to destroy the antigens.

Antigens: substances that can stimulate an immune response. Antigens induce the formation of antibodies by the immune system, then react specifically with those antibodies. Some antigens, such as bacteria and viruses, are foreign substances introduced into the body. Others are harmful substances formed within the body. Still others are cells or other substances normally found within the body, which for some reason are recognized as "foreign" and attacked by the immune system.

Atherosclerosis: a condition in which fat deposits build up in the walls of the arteries. Atherosclerosis can interfere with the flow of blood in the arteries, resulting in heart attacks, strokes, and other health problems.

Beta cells: the insulin-producing cells located in the islets of Langerhans.

Cholesterol: a fatlike substance found in blood and other tissues in people and animals. Too much cholesterol in the blood can speed the buildup of fat in the walls of the arteries, slowing the flow of blood and contributing to heart and blood-vessel disease.

Coma: a state of unconsciousness. Among the causes of coma are blood sugar levels that are too high or too low.

Complications: certain diseases or conditions that may arise during a disease such as diabetes. The acute (sudden and short-lasting) complications of diabetes include insulin reactions and ketoacidosis; the chronic complications (those that develop slowly and are long-lasting) include diseases of the eyes, kidneys, blood vessels, and nerves.

Delta cells: the somatostatin-producing cells in the islets of Langerhans.

Diabetes: a general term for disorders in which the body produces too much urine.

Diabetes insipidus: a disease usually caused by lack of a hormone produced by the pituitary gland. People with diabetes insipidus secrete large amounts of urine, but the urine is sugar-free.

Diabetes mellitus: a disease that develops when the pancreas doesn't make enough insulin, or the body cannot use the insulin it has. People with diabetes mellitus cannot use sugar for energy in the normal way. If the diabetes is uncontrolled, they have high blood sugar levels and secrete large amounts of sugary urine.

DNA (deoxyribonucleic acid): a chemical substance carried in the chromosomes of the body cells. DNA carries the hereditary blueprint (genes) for making insulin and other body proteins.

Enzyme: a type of protein that is produced by living cells and helps in various body functions.

Gene: a basic unit of heredity; a segment of DNA that carries hereditary information in coded form. For example, the insulin gene directs the beta cells to make insulin.

Glucagon: a hormone produced by the alpha cells of the islets of Langerhans. Glucagon helps raise blood sugar levels.

Glucose: a simple sugar that acts as the body's main source of energy.

Glycogen: the form in which sugar is stored in the liver and muscles.

Glycosuria (glucosuria): sugar in the urine.

Glycosylated hemoglobin test: a blood test performed in the doctor's office to measure the average blood sugar level over a several-month period.

HLA antigens: certain proteins on the surface of the body cells. Like other antigens, HLA antigens normally help the immune system distinguish between the body's own tissues and foreign tissues. HLA-DR3 and -DR4 antigens are thought to play a role in the development of Type I.

Hormone: a substance that is secreted by a gland and circulates in the bloodstream, producing an effect elsewhere in the body.

Human genome: the complete set of instructions for creating a human being; the information contained in the DNA in the chromosomes of each of the body cells.

Hyperglycemia: a blood sugar level that is higher than normal.

Hypoglycemia: a blood sugar level that is lower than normal.

Hypoglycemic drugs: see oral hypoglycemic drugs.

Insulin: a hormone produced by the beta cells in the islets of Langerhans. Insulin is the "key" that helps sugar enter the body cells, where it is used for energy.

Insulin-dependent diabetes mellitus (IDDM): see Type I diabetes.

Insulin reaction: occurs when there is too low a level of blood sugar (usually below 50 mg/dL) in a diabetic person who is taking insulin. The reaction is caused by too much insulin, too little food, too much exercise, or other factors.

Insulin receptor sites: places on the cell wall where insulin binds and glucose enters the cell; the "keyhole" into which insulin fits.

Islets: see islets of Langerhans.

Islets of Langerhans: groups of cells scattered throughout the pancreas. The islets contain several types of cells, among them the beta cells, the alpha cells, and the delta cells.

Ketoacidosis: a dangerous condition in which ketones build up in the blood and spill into the urine. Ketoacidosis occurs when blood sugar levels get too high and the body breaks down fats for energy.

Ketones: waste products formed when fats are broken down for energy.

(117)

Ketonuria: the presence of ketones in the urine.

mg/dL: milligrams per deciliter. One milligram is one-thousandth of a gram, and one deciliter is one-tenth of a liter.

Non-insulin-dependent diabetes mellitus (NIDDM): see Type II diabetes.

Oral hypoglycemic drugs: drugs that some patients with Type II diabetes take by mouth to help lower blood sugar levels. Oral hypoglycemic drugs do not contain insulin, and are effective only if the body is able to produce some insulin.

Pancreas: a large gland behind the stomach that secretes a digestive juice into the small intestine. It also contains groups of different cells, including the beta cells, which produce the hormone insulin.

Pituitary gland: a small, oval gland near the base of the brain, which secretes hormones that influence body growth and metabolism.

Polydipsia: excessive thirst.

Polyphagia: escessive appetite or eating.

Polyuria: frequent urination.

Type I diabetes (insulin-dependent diabetes mellitus): the type of diabetes in which the pancreas produces little or no insulin. People with Type I need insulin injections in order to live.

Type II diabetes (non-insulin-dependent diabetes mellitus): the type of diabetes in which the body may produce small or large amounts of insulin, but doesn't use the insulin effectively.

FOR ADDITIONAL READING

The American Diabetes Association. *Diabetes in the Family.* Bowie, Md.: Robert J. Brady Co., 1987.

The American Diabetes Association and The American Dietetic Association. *Family Cookbook: Volume III.* New York: Prentice-Hall Press, 1987.

Bliss, Michael. *The Discovery of Insulin.* University of Chicago Press, 1982.

Cantu, Robert C. *Diabetes and Exercise.* New York: E. P. Dutton, 1982.

Harris, Seale. *Banting's Miracle: The Story of the Discoverer of Insulin.* Philadelphia: J. B. Lippincott Company, 1946.

Wrenshall, G. A. *The Story of Insulin: Forty Years of Success Against Diabetes.* Bloomington: Indiana University Press, 1964.

ORGANIZATIONS TO CONTACT

The organizations listed below sponsor educational programs and provide information on diabetes. Call or write for a publication list, order form, and other information.

American Diabetes Association
National Service Center
1660 Duke Street
Alexandria, VA 22314
1-800-ADA-DISC
(Virginia and metropolitan D.C.: 1-703-549-1500)

ADA funds research, conducts professional education programs, and provides services like summer camp and support groups for all people with diabetes. A twenty-four-dollar annual membership in ADA includes membership in a local chapter and a subscription to *Diabetes Forecast* (monthly). *Diabetes 90*, a free quarterly newsletter, is available to nonmembers by calling the toll-free number. State or local chapters provide information on summer camps for diabetic children.

National Diabetes Information Clearinghouse
Box NDIC
Bethesda, MD 20892
301-468-2162

NDIC maintains an extensive online data base and responds to inquiries about diabetes. The Clearinghouse also offers a free newsletter, *Diabetes Dateline*.

International Diabetes Center
5000 West 39th Street
Minneapolis, MN 55416
612-927-3393

The IDC provides on-site health-care services in Minneapolis and brings together diabetic patients and specialized health-care providers at centers throughout the world.

Juvenile Diabetes Foundation International
The Diabetes Research Foundation
432 Park Avenue South
New York, NY 10016
1-800-JDF-CURE

A twenty-five-dollar annual membership in JDF includes a subscription to *Countdown* (quarterly). The Foundation supports diabetes research and responds to inquiries about diabetes.

Joslin Diabetes Center
One Joslin Place
Boston, MA 02215
617-732-2415

The Joslin Diabetes Center provides complete medical and educational services for people with diabetes, including summer camps for diabetic children. A twenty-five-dollar annual membership includes a subscription to *Joslin* magazine (quarterly).

INDEX

Fiber, 65, 67
Fish, 26, 65, 68
Foot care, 95–97
Foot damage, 60, 95, *96*, 97, 100
Fruits, 65, 67, 68
Future, and diabetes, 105–113

Gangrene, 95, *96*
Gene(s), 39, 42, 109; manipulation, 111–113
Gestational diabetes, *43*, 44
Glucagon, 27, 29, 91, 98
Glucometer, *58*
Glucose, 9–10, 13, 65, 73; impaired glucose tolerance, 44; metabolism, 26–29; plasma glucose tests, 46–48. *See also* Blood sugar levels
Glycemic index, 69
Glycogen, 13, 27
Glycosuria, 33
Glycosylated hemoglobin test, 59–60

Health professionals, 51, 59, 61, 95, 97, 99, 102
Heart disease, 31, 52, 60, 66, 68, 73, 100
Hemoglobin, 60
Hereditary factors, 36, 37, 39, 40, 42, 44, 102, 109; gene manipulation, 111–113
High blood pressure, 59, 68
History of diabetes, 11–23
HLA antigens, 41, 112
Hormones, 9, 16, 19, 25,

Hormones (*continued*)
27–29, 51, 61. *See also* Insulin
Human Biological Data Interchange, 109
Human genome, 112–113
Human insulin, 81
Hyperglycemia, 33
Hypoglycemia, 89–90

Identification, 98
Illness, diabetic care during, 99
Immune factors, 40–42
Immune system, 41–42, 107–108, 112
Immunosuppressive drugs, 107–108
Impaired glucose tolerance, 44
Implantable insulin pumps, 106–107
Impotence, 52, 60
Increase in diabetic cases, 105
Infections, 40, 41, 60, 95–97, 107
Injection sites, 83, 84–88
Insulin, 9–10, 14, 16; administration of, 81–88, 106–107; discovery of, 18–23; lack of, 29–31, 36; normal role of, 26–27; sources of, 79–81; therapy, 18–23, 35, 37, 49, 50, 51, 53, 59, 71, 79–88, 99, 106–107, 111; and Type I diabetes, 35, 36, 79–88, 111; and Type II diabetes, 36–37, 42, 44, 79